Educational Anthropology: An Introduction

The Educational Philosophy of National Socialism (Yale)
The Education of the Mexican Nation (Columbia)
Higher Learning in Britain (California)
Existentialism and Education (Philosophical Library)
Foundations of Education (Wiley)
Introduction to the Philosophy of Education (Wiley)
Educational Anthropology: An Introduction (Wiley)
The Art and Science of Creativity (Holt)

Educational Anthropology:
AN INTRODUCTION

George F. Kneller
University of California, Los Angeles

JOHN WILEY & SONS, INC., NEW YORK · LONDON · SYDNEY

Library of Congress Catalog Card Number: 65-14252
Printed in the United States of America

For John and Evelina
sine quibus non...

Preface

The idea of a union of education and anthropology first caught my imagination some twenty-five years ago when my studies of education in National Socialist Germany brought me to grips with questions of race and culture. My mentor then was Bronislaw Malinowski. As it happened, our conferences proved mutually beneficial, for in helping me see the potential fruitfulness of anthropology for education, he himself came to appreciate better what education could contribute to his own subject.

I realized the value of such a union more keenly in 1942 when I conducted a full-scale survey of Mexican education for the United States government. After spending several months in the Indian communities of Mexico, I found that the historical, philosophic, and political approaches I was accustomed to take to comparative studies no longer sufficed. The diversity of Mexican education could be understood only in terms of conflicting cultures, which education at last was beginning to fuse. In this survey I had the invaluable aid of two anthropologists epitomizing opposite points of view: Pablo Martínez del Río, a conservative Roman Catholic, and Manuel Gamio, a liberal social reformer. I also learned from Robert Redfield that not only factual studies but also bold generalizations were needed to harness anthropology to the study of education. Upon my return to Yale, I profited from the wisdom of Ralph Linton to write *The Education of the Mexican Nation* (Columbia University Press, 1951).

Now, in this text I apply the tools of anthropology to American education itself. Two decades have been a long time for me to wait, but I hope that my activities in the meantime have broadened and deepened the resources I bring to this subject. Of the risks involved I am well aware, for I have set out to do what few have attempted—namely, to expound systematically the main points of contact between the disciplines of education, in particular American education, and cultural anthropology.

If this book helps, however modestly, to excite the interest of students in the growing study of educational anthropology, and if it fertilizes inquiring minds with ideas for research, it will have served its purpose and amply repaid the labor of writing.

To anthropologists Ruth Landes, Councill Taylor, and Wendell Oswalt, who read this manuscript with care and insight, I must express enduring gratitude. Without their perceptive commentaries this book would have been much the poorer.

GEORGE F. KNELLER

Los Angeles, California
November 1964

Contents

1

Anthropology, Culture, Education

THE MEANING OF ANTHROPOLOGY

Anthropology is the study of man and his ways of living. It has two main branches: physical anthropology, which traces the evolution of the human organism and its adaptation to different environments; and cultural anthropology, which is the study of cultures living and dead. At its broadest, cultural anthropology includes linguistics (the study of speech forms), archaeology (the study of dead cultures), and ethnology, which is the study of living cultures or those that can be observed directly.[1] Our concern is the relation of education to cultural anthropology in this last sense.

Anthropology became a science about a century ago in the ferment of ideas stimulated by exploration, archaelogy, geology, and, above all, Darwinism. Influenced by the concept of organic evolution, the first English and American anthropologists, such as Edward Burnett Tylor and Lewis Henry Morgan, regarded all cultures as stages on a single highway leading to the societies of industrial Europe and America. Morgan, for instance, posited three necessary phases of cultural growth—savagery, barbarism, and civilization—with their appropriate substages.

---

[1] Culture and society imply each other, for without living together men cannot create a culture or way of life, and without a way of life they cannot live together. I shall define and distinguish culture and society shortly.

1

On the Continent, by contrast, the *Kulturkreislehre* or "culture-diffusion school" maintained that cultures were the result not of independent parallel growth, but rather of the diffusion of inventions from a few cultural centers. Both schools, however, with their broad theoretical sweep and their assumption of an increasing complexity in culture equivalent to universal progress, bred an inevitable reaction. Emile Durkheim on the Continent, Franz Boas in America, and Bronislaw Malinowski in England each initiated an anthropological empiricism, substituting for the study of mankind as a whole the painstaking examination of particular cultures. Malinowski, for instance, founded the school of *functionalism*, which largely turned from the traditional study of the history of cultures in order to explain each facet of a culture in terms of its contribution to the whole at a given moment.[2]

Although nonhistorical functionalism took hold of British anthropology, Boas's historical relativism influenced most American anthropologists, especially Edward Sapir, Ruth Benedict, and Melville J. Herskovits.[3] In the 1930's anthropology was broadened and deepened by a new interest, pioneered by Ruth Benedict, in the concept of *cultures as wholes*. Whereas Boas in the main had considered the individual parts of different cultures, certain of his successors turned their attention to the basic *patterns* or *configurations* of parts that make each culture a functioning whole. Since then, the major innovation has been the study of *culture-and-personality*, that is, of the process by which culture is internalized and modified by the individual person—a trend that has tempered the anthropologist's tendency to be overconcerned with culture

---

[2] Bronislaw Malinowski, *A Scientific Theory of Culture and Other Essays*, University of North Carolina Press, Raleigh, 1944, p. 118, rejects the idea that the origins of the fork, for example, can be explained historically: "The only intelligent hypothesis is that the origins of the fork are the performance of the minimum tasks which the instrument can perform." See also A. R. Radcliffe-Brown, *A Natural Science of Society*, Free Press of Glencoe, New York, 1957, p. 85: "Function may be defined as the total set of relations that a single social activity or usage or belief has to the total system." (Malinowski, however, had more use for history than most functionalists. In his early studies of the Trobriand Islanders he used little history because little history was available. In his later African studies history became more important.)
[3] Historical relativism is the study of particular cultures in terms of their past as well as their present experience.

per se rather than with the individuals who make it possible.[4]

Although it is among the youngest of the social sciences, anthropology surpasses the rest in the range of its subject matter and methodology. Whereas other scholars study certain aspects of a culture, the anthropologist seeks to relate all aspects to the culture as a whole; whereas they concentrate on certain advanced cultures of the industrial West, he turns to all cultures, past and present, primitive and civilized; whereas they take into account particular stretches of the past, he takes for his province the whole history of mankind. Above all, the anthropologist makes us aware of the sheer diversity of cultures and of the deep impress of cultural conditioning on human behavior and personality. He shows us how much, or how little, human nature can be altered.

Yet this great scope proves to be not only a strength but also a weakness, for it makes anthropology the least ordered of the sciences, with no accepted core of theory permitting wide and accurate prediction. Moreover, the focus on culture, which is the main source of this scope, has another limitation. Since all cultural experiences must be shared by at least two persons and are shared as a rule by many, anthropology understands groups better than it does persons. It does not go deep into individual human nature, least of all into the unconscious.[5] To understand such depths, we must look elsewhere—in religion, psychology, the drama, and the novel. Anthropology, then, contributes to, but does not subsume, the study of man.[6]

---

[4] Recent years have seen a revival of the evolutionary approach to the study of cultures, although anthropologists do not yet agree that it constitutes a significant contemporary school. See Marshall Sahlins and Elman R. Service, eds., *Evolution and Culture*, University of Michigan Press, Ann Arbor, 1960; and *Evolution and Anthropology: A Centennial Appraisal*, Anthropological Society of Washington, Washington, D.C., 1959. See also Elizabeth E. Hoyt, "Integration of Culture: A Review of Concepts," *Current Anthropology*, II, No. 5 (December 1961), 407–426.

[5] Cf. Robert Redfield, "Anthropology's Contribution to the Understanding of Man," *Anthropological Quarterly*, Redfield Commemorative Issue, XXXII, No. 1 (January 1959), 4.

[6] Cf. Clyde Kluckhohn, *Mirror for Man: The Relation of Anthrolopogy to Modern Life*, Whittlesey House, New York, 1949, p. 1: "Present-day anthropology . . . cannot pretend to be the whole study of man, though perhaps it comes closer than any other branch of science."

THE MEANING OF CULTURE

By *culture as such* we mean all the ways of life that have been evolved by men in society. By a *particular culture* we mean the total shared way of life of a given people, comprising their modes of thinking, acting, and feeling, which are expressed, for instance, in religion, law, language, art, and custom, as well as in material products, such as houses, clothes, and tools. From another perspective we may regard a culture as the learned and shared behavior (thoughts, acts, and feelings) of a certain people together with their artifacts—learned in the sense that this behavior is transmitted socially rather than genetically, shared in that it is practiced either by the whole population or by some part of it.

Our culture is the way we eat and sleep, the way we wash and dress and go to work. It is the actions we perform at home and on the job. It is the language we speak and the values and beliefs we hold. It is the goods and services we buy and the way we buy them. It is the way we meet friends and strangers, the way we control our children and the way they respond. It is the transportation we use and the entertainment we enjoy.

How, then, is *culture* to be distinguished from *society*? A society is a localized population that cooperates over a period of time for certain ends; a culture is this society's way of life, or the things that its members think and feel and do. As Felix Keesing says, "Put most simply, 'culture' puts the focus on the customs of a people; 'society' puts it on the people who are practicing the customs." [7] Animals and insects, it is true, also live in societies; indeed, some, such as deer herds, have "families" and "leaders." But such social behavior is instinctual rather than learned and, hence, it has not given rise to culture.

Is a single society coterminous with a single culture? It probably is, provided the society is small, isolated, and stable. Most large societies, however, are multicultural or pluralist. They tend to have several or many subcultures. The United States, for instance, contains the subcultures of Indians, Mexicans, Puerto Ricans, the armed forces, adolescents, jazz musicians, and others.

---

[7] Felix M. Keesing, *Cultural Anthropology: The Science of Custom*, Rinehart, New York, 1958, p. 30.

The Content of Culture

The phenomena of culture can be ordered in a number of ways. They may, for instance, be classified as learned and shared *activities*, such as driving, dating, and going to the theater; learned and shared *ideas*, such as belief in God and hostility to communism; and shared and socially acquired *artifacts*, such as automobiles and skyscrapers. Phenomena may also be classified as *technology* (the means by which a culture manipulates the material world), *social organization* (the activities and institutions involved in the behavior of its members with one another), and *ideology* (the culture's knowledge, values, and beliefs).[8] One of the best known classifications is Ralph Linton's triad of *universals*, *specialties*, and *alternatives*.[9] Universals are whatever thoughts, acts, feelings, and artifacts are common to all adults in a society. They include, among other things, language, housing, kinship relations, clothing, and various beliefs and values. Specialties are those phenomena shared only by members of certain socially recognized groups, such as the skilled trades and professions. Alternatives are those which are shared by a limited number of individuals, such as priests, painters, or philosophers.

But a culture is more than the sum of its parts; it is also the way that those parts are organized to form a whole. Just as several buildings can be made of the same materials yet differ in structure and function, so various cultures may share some similar elements yet each may organize them uniquely. Thus, to understand a culture we must grasp not only its parts but also the structure that holds them.

According to anthropologists, this structure consists of certain basic *configurations*, generally corresponding to the culture's fundamental attitudes and beliefs. Some anthropologists have sought to characterize each culture by a single configuration. Ruth Benedict, for example, contrasts the Dionysian *ethos* (or configuration) of the Indians of the Western Plains, who value excess,

---

[8] Cf. John J. Honigmann, *The World of Man*, Harper, New York, 1959, pp. 288–289.
[9] Ralph Linton, *The Study of Man*, Appleton-Century, New York, 1936, pp. 272–287.

with the Apollonian ethos of the Pueblo Indians, who esteem moderation.[10] Most anthropologists, however, prefer to look for a number of configurations, at least in more complex societies. Some of the configurations may be dominant whereas others may be supportive or even conflicting.[11]

Organized about such configurations, each culture forms an *interdependent system* whose coherence is felt rather than rationally constructed. These configurations interpenetrate all sectors of the culture. As Ruth Benedict observes, "All the miscellaneous behavior directed toward getting a living, mating, warring, and worshipping the gods, is made over into consistent patterns in accordance with unconscious canons of choice that develop deep within the culture." [12] Opler, for instance, shows that among the Chiricahua Apache the "theme" of male predominance is manifested in a range of beliefs, such as the belief that a vigorous fetus will be a boy and the belief that women, being less stable than men, are more likely to cause strife in the home. It is expressed, too, in such customs as the restriction of tribal councils to men and the practice of assigning special places at feasts for men, allowing the women to eat where they can.[13]

Being systematic, culture is also *selective*, innovating and adapting according to its underlying configurations. Clyde Kluckhohn and William H. Kelly make this point very well:

Just as the choice of an individual at a critical epoch commits him in certain directions for the rest of his life, so the original bents, trends, "interests" which become established in the design for living of a newly

---

[10] Ruth Benedict, *Patterns of Culture*, Houghton Mifflin, Boston, 1934. Benedict's single configurations have been widely criticised, however, even as applied to primitive cultures. See, for example, H. Driver, *Indians of North America*, University of Chicago, 1961, pp. 519 ff.

[11] In addition to Benedict's *ethos*, alternative terms for configuration include Herskovits' *sanction* and Opler's *theme*. See Melville J. Herskovits, *Cultural Anthropology*, Knopf, New York, 1955, p. 425: "The underlying drives, motivations, 'unconscious system of meanings' that govern the reactions of a people can be thought of as the sanctions of their culture." See also M. E. Opler, "Themes as Dynamic Forces in Culture," *American Journal of Sociology*, LI, No. 3 (November 1945), 198–200.

[12] Ruth Benedict, *Patterns of Culture*, Houghton Mifflin, Boston, 1934, p. 48.

[13] M. E. Opler, "Themes as Dynamic Forces in Culture," *American Journal of Sociology*, LI, No. 3 (November 1945), 198–200.

formed society tend to channel a culture in some directions as opposed to others. Subsequent variations on the culture—both those which arise internally and those which are a response to contact with other cultures or to changes in the natural environment—are not random. In some sense, at least, there is probably cultural orthogenesis as well as biological orthogenesis.[14]

The anthropological term for the degree of unity achieved by a culture is *integration*. Every culture contains a multitude of different patterns of behavior. American culture, for instance, includes such patterns as brushing the teeth, watching television, playing baseball, and electing a president. Now, a culture is integrated to the extent that its patterns of behavior are interrelated. The more integrated the culture, the more these patterns reinforce one another. The less integrated the culture, the more they function independently. Related patterns of behavior also form more embracing patterns, or subsystems, within the total system of the culture. Thus, such behavior patterns as learning to read, raising one's hand in class, correcting papers, and attending teacher's colleges all belong to the subsystem of education.

In every culture some subsystems are more important than others. The most important subsystems are known to anthropologists as *foci*. A focus is an area of great interest and concern to the culture's members. It is an assemblage of behavior patterns that absorbs much of their time and energy. The more integrated the culture, the more its foci dominate its patterns of behavior and the more these foci are related to one another. The converse is true of less integrated cultures.[15]

The Hopi, for example, are a highly integrated culture. Among the Hopi two foci—ceremonial participation and social life—in one way or other embrace most of the culture's activities. Ceremonial participation includes such varied activities as secret societies, marriage arrangements and rituals, the cult of the *kachina*

---

14 Clyde Kluckhohn and William H. Kelly, "The Concept of Culture," in Ralph Linton, ed., *The Science of Man in the World Crisis*, Columbia University Press, New York, 1945, p. 96.
15 The term *focus* was coined by Melville J. Herskovits. It is similar in meaning to configuration, except that it refers to a dominant subsystem of related behavior patterns, whereas *configuration* refers generally to a guiding belief or value.

(spiritual beings venerated by the Hopi), and subsistence. In order to understand these activities, one must see how they are interrelated within the focus of ceremonial participation.[16]

American culture is less integrated. Two of this culture's many foci are education and the factory system. Were American culture more highly integrated, the curriculum would be more directly geared to the needs of industry than it is at present, and business interests would exercise more initiative in sponsoring educational developments. A totalitarian society is naturally more integrated than a democracy, because it can impose more order on its culture. Thus, in Russia, under the name of "polytechnization" education is related more directly to the needs of industry than it is in this country. [17]

The more tightly knit the culture, the greater its resistance to change, since even its seemingly casual traits are intimately grounded in its guiding foci or configurations. If the change is enforced, the culture may be seriously affected and may even collapse.[18] The Samoan culture, for instance, was disrupted by the introduction of Western-style houses which lacked the posts indicating the seating positions of persons of different ranks.[19] Then there is the case of a North Australian tribe whose men used the stone ax to kill animals and cut firewood. The ax was their

---

[16] On the integration of the Hopi, see Mischa Titiev, *Old Oraibi*, Papers of the Peabody Museum of American Archaeology and Ethnology, XXII, No. 1, Cambridge, Mass.

[17] An introductory textbook seeking to combine two disciplines must simplify heavily. Here as elsewhere I am forced to condense greatly a complicated anthropological topic in order to make it intelligible to students of education in the space available. For a fuller treatment of the subject of integration the reader is referred to John Gillin, *The Ways of Men*, Appleton-Century-Crofts, New York, 1948, pp. 517–520; and Wendell Oswalt, *Napaskiak: An Alaskan Eskimo Community*, University of Arizona Press, Tucson, 1963, pp. 150–153.

[18] H. G. Barnett et al., "Acculturation: An Exploratory Formulation," *American Anthropologist*, LVI, No. 6 (December 1954), 986: "Under coercion the receptive culture . . . loses its freedom to modify creatively what it is forced to accept as given. This strait-jacketing of acceptance forbids the flexibility of reinterpretation and reassociation that is essential to the independent functioning of a cultural system."

[19] Clyde Kluckhohn, *Mirror for Man*, Whittlesey House, New York, 1949, p. 187.

treasured possession and the symbol of their masculinity. Missionaries, however, introduced steel choppers and gave them to both men and women. Quite unintentionally they disturbed the pattern of sex and age relationships, destroying the reasons that led children and adolescents to obey their male elders and depriving the men of their self-respect. Now women could chop! The tribe was almost ruined by an act of kindness![20]

Conversely, the more loosely integrated the culture, the more readily it can absorb a range of innovations without immediately threatening its own foundations. Thus, the eclectic cultures of the West have received algebra from the Arabs, printing from the Chinese, tobacco from America, and countless other innovations from cultures throughout the world.

No culture, however, is ever wholly integrated. Integration, as A. L. Kroeber says, "is an ideal condition invented by a few anthropologists not versed in history." [21] Most areas of a culture possess a measure of autonomy, but precisely how much varies considerably from one culture to another and within the same culture from one area to another. For example, even in the most flexible cultures grammar remains fairly constant whereas vocabularly is constantly changing.

Since integration is never complete and since culture is not rationally planned but rather the product of a long and complex history, every culture contains inconsistencies and inefficiencies. For example, our own culture uses undecimalized weights and measures and a spelling at variance with pronunciation, both of which usages are at odds with our concern for efficiency.

Some Characteristics of Culture

Culture is both *organic* and *supraorganic*. It is organic in being rooted ultimately in the human organism, since without people to

---

[20] For the problem of acculturation, see Laura Thompson, *Culture in Crisis,* University of Chicago Press, 1950; Clyde Kluckhohn and Dorothea Leighton, *The Navaho,* Harvard University Press, Cambridge, 1946; Sol Tax, ed., *Acculturation in the Americas, Proceedings and Selected Papers of the XXIXth International Congress of Americanists* (n.d.), especially A. Irving Hallowell, "Ojibwa Personality and Acculturation," pp. 105–112.

[21] A. L. Kroeber, *The Nature of Culture,* University of Chicago Press, 1952, p. 130.

act, think, feel, and make artifacts there would be no culture at all. It is supraorganic in the sense that it outlives particular generations and that its content is more a product of human society than of human biology.

Culture is *overt* and *covert*. It is overt in those actions and artifacts, such as houses, clothes, and speech forms, that can be observed directly; and covert in those aspects, such as its underlying attitude toward nature and the world of the spirit, that must be inferred from what its members say and do.

Culture is *explicit* and *implicit*. Explicit culture consists of all those modes of behavior, such as driving a car, making love, and playing baseball, that can be described readily by those who perform them. Implicit culture comprises those things that people more or less take for granted and that they cannot easily explain. For instance, all sane adults can speak their culture's language but few can explain its grammar and syntax in any detail.

Culture is *ideal* and *manifest*. Ideal culture comprises the ways in which a people believe they ought to behave, or in which they would like to behave, or in which they believe they *do* behave. Manifest culture consists of their actual behavior. Thus, Christianity in the United States is now more ideal than manifest. Many Americans, if questioned, would acknowledge a vague belief in an afterlife, but relatively few in their daily lives take practical steps to prepare for it. In cultures undergoing rapid change the gap between ideal and manifest culture is almost certain to widen, for, as a rule, changing conditions, especially changing technology, swiftly outpace ideals. Contrast our ideal of "rugged individualism" with the actual domination of the economy by a relatively small number of large firms.

Culture is *stable* yet always *changing*. Logically, indeed, each quality implies the other, for change can be measured only against elements that are relatively stable, and stability against those that change more swiftly. Some cultures, those of the West especially, are more flexible than others and can adjust to a swifter rate of change without disintegrating. In addition, a culture is more receptive to change in some of its aspects than in others. In Western cultures, for instance, technology changes more swiftly than values. Nevertheless, neither values nor ideology remain wholly static. Few Americans, for instance, any longer accept the account of Creation in Genesis as literally true. All anthropologists in general emphasize the fundamental mutability of culture,[22] although a minority, such as Leslie White and some modern evolutionists, emphasize the resistance of culture to deliberate and rationally conceived attempts at cultural change.[23]

Thus far I have outlined the meaning, content, and general characteristics of culture; I have introduced the reader to the basic language, as it were, in which anthropological knowledge is communicated. Let us now survey the ground relation between anthropology and education.

EDUCATION AND ANTHROPOLOGY

In its widest sense, education includes every process, except the solely genetic, that helps to form a person's mind, character, or physical capacity. It is life-long, for we must learn new ways of thought and action with every major change in our lives.[24] More narrowly, education is the inculcation in each generation of certain knowledge, skills, and attitudes by means of institutions, such as schools, deliberately created for this end. Yet again, the term *education* also stands for the academic discipline (including the psychology, sociology, history, and philosophy of education) whose subject is education in the second sense.

Man seems always to have known that the young do not mature culturally unless they are shown how. Children, too, realize that the techniques of adulthood must be learned from their elders. Every society has discovered that the transmission of its culture

---

22 E.g. Melville J. Herskovits, "The Processes of Cultural Change," in Ralph Linton, ed., *The Science of Man in the World Crisis*, Columbia University Press, New York, 1945, pp. 143–170.
23 See p. 20, and cf. Marshall D. Sahlins and Elman R. Service, eds., *Evolution and Culture*, University of Michigan Press, Ann Arbor, 1960, pp. 53–68.
24 Bronislaw Malinowski, *Freedom and Civilization*, Allen and Unwin, London, 1947, p. 141:

> Taking education in its widest sense, we see readily that it is a process which lasts through life. Every new status which an individual acquires, every new condition of life, such as marriage, parenthood, maturity, and old age, have to be learned, in that the individual has to adjust gradually and by the acquisition of new attitudes, new ideas, and also new social duties and responsibilities.

cannot be left to chance. Granted that the child absorbs this culture from the countless experiences of this daily life, yet such informal assimilation cannot guarantee that he receives precisely those elements of culture that society believes its members must have if they are to perpetuate and renew it. Every society, therefore, supervises the education of its members. At some point in his childhood everyone is formally educated, though not necessarily in a school.

Education, then, belongs to the general process known as *enculturation*, by which the growing person is initiated into the way of life of his society. To understand the dynamics of enculturation as they affect education, we must turn to anthropology. Let one example suffice. Cultures, we know, vary in the degree of *discontinuity* that they impose between childhood and maturity. In some cultures the ascent to adulthood is smooth and unbroken; in others, such as our own, the adolescent is required abruptly to reorient his way of life with resultant stress and strain. This state of affairs raises questions of great importance to education. How much discontinuity is inevitable for anyone who grows up in a modern industrial society? How much can be alleviated? How does this discontinuity affect school studies and methods of instruction?

But education considered as schooling is only one of a number of enculturating agencies—in particular the family, the church, the peer group, and the mass media—each with its own values and purposes. Thus, although the educator may want to cultivate certain qualities in the child, such as clear thinking and independent judgment, he is limited in his ability to do so by the fact that other agencies may be molding the child differently.[25] Tele-

---

[25] Margaret Mead makes the point more dramatically:

In small societies children learn by imitating their parents, relatives, and neighbors. In our huge society we use our mass entertainments to instruct our children on how they should express their emotions and what values they should have. . . . We are showing our youngsters exactly the opposite of what we want them to imitate. We are showing them men who brutally attack others when angry. We show people who murder because of hatred and expediency. We show that love is expressed only by hunger for another's body. And we show them little else.

Margaret Mead, "The Educative Environment," *The News Letter*, Bureau of Educational Research and Service, Ohio State University, Columbus, Edgar Dale and Hazel Gibbony, eds., XXVI, No. 8 (May 1961), 2.

vision, for instance, seeks occasionally to inform but mainly to amuse, sometimes to thrill, and constantly to sell through insinuation, assertion, and persuasion. Can it by such means produce lucid and independent minds? How far can the school cooperate with other enculturating agencies, and how far must it oppose them? To what extent are these agencies at odds with one another, and to what extent are they allies of the school? In order to answer these questions and to devise appropriate policies for the school, the educator must know the nature and scope of the enculturating agencies. For this he must turn to anthropology.

As one sector in the great network of culture, education reacts to events in other parts of the culture and may on occasion affect these events itself. In an industrial culture one of the great engines of change is science and its application in technology. We in the Western world are living in what has been called the second industrial revolution. The first, pivoting upon the steam engine and the spinning machine, replaced muscle with machinery. The second has gathered momentum since 1945, although it began earlier in the century. Revolving around atomic power, chemicals, computers, and automation, it has vastly increased the energy that we can produce and is beginning to substitute machines for human thought and control.

Far more than the first, this revolution relies on the expert—on the technician and the professional—rather than on the cultivated amateur. It has affected our schools and colleges profoundly by committing them to technical and professional specialization. An increasingly specialized society also affects the profession of education, creating growing numbers of administrators, counselors, researchers, testers, and other experts. In its turn education raises the level and rate of change in science and technology by producing more, and more highly trained, scientists and technologists.

In such a society—complex, specialized, and swiftly changing—the school's task of cultural transmission is increasingly beset with problems. The volume of knowledge is vast already and continually growing, and there is no general agreement on what the pupil should learn. At the same time, this knowledge is becoming ever more specialized, with the result that the pupil must learn more, both to master his specialty and to comprehend the culture as a whole. Moreover, the fact of rapid and continuous change makes it difficult to predict what the next generation should know.

Thus, as the number of things to be learned increases, either the time spent on learning each one must diminish, or better methods of learning and teaching must be invented, or both. There seems little doubt, however, that despite the range of teaching methods already devised to communicate different subjects, modern man is amassing knowledge faster than he is inventing methods to communicate it. And a new method to communicate new knowledge, if there should be one, implies an additional subject to be learned, as in the case of automated instruction.[26]

In order, then, to understand what our school system is capable of achieving and in what ways cultural factors are frustrating it, we must see education within the context of culture as a whole. Here educator and anthropologist must collaborate, for as a rule the educator lacks the anthropologist's acquaintance with the sweep and detail of culture, whereas few anthropologists are likely to turn their attention to the cultural phenomenon of education alone.

In particular, the anthropologist can trace those conflicts in the wider culture that permeate the whole subculture of education and of which the practicing educator generally is unaware. For instance, the conflict between traditional American values and the emerging values of an affluent society frequently crowns the actions of the teacher with results that he never intended. If we are to insure that education attains its acknowledged goals, we need the anthropologist to tell us where the internalized antagonisms of the culture are thwarting the teacher's efforts.

Since its first task is to perpetuate the achievements of the culture, education is fundamentally conservative. Yet, to the extent that it prepares the young to adapt to happenings anticipated both inside and outside the culture, it paves the way for cultural change. Can education do more than this? Can it train the coming generation not merely to adapt to, but also to initiate specific changes in the culture? Once again, to answer this controversial question, we must turn to anthropology in order to discover the gamut of forces that the culture brings to bear on its educational system. Any sensible plan for making the school a spearhead of

---

[26] Cf. Jules Henry, "A Cross-Cultural Outline of Education," *Current Anthropology*, I, No. 4 (July 1960), 270–271, 283.

cultural change must take into account the forces that the school is up against.

Anthropology can also contribute to education by studying the educational methods of other cultures, both primitive and modern. A cross-cultural study of education enables the educator to learn from the experiences of other cultures and to examine his own schools more objectively. Although it remains to be seen whether a system of categories can be devised applicable to the educational systems of all cultures, the attempt must be made.[27] The educator must proceed carefully, however, for cultures, being unique, are difficult to compare. Moreover, categories of comparison must be tentative, since new ones are bound to appear.

At the moment, scholars are engaged in a series of case studies of the cultural factors at work in a range of educational situations.[28] Yet, although some notable contributions have been made, the examination of the interplay of culture and education has barely begun. Whether the time is ripe for a comprehensive theory of educational anthropology is, perhaps, open to dispute. Theodore Brameld has already essayed such a theory. Grandly conceived and impressively worked out, it nevertheless illuminates the educational process chiefly in accordance with Brameld's philosophy of reconstructionism, which I shall discuss later.[29] George D. Spindler, on the other hand, advocates a more inductive approach. He maintains that the chief contribution anthropology can make to education is to put together a body of verified, empirical knowledge by analyzing different aspects of the educational process in its sociocultural milieu.[30]

Yet, special theories and separate experiments will not in themselves develop a discipline of educational anthropology. At bottom, educational anthropology must be a systematic study, not only of the practice of education in cultural perspective, but also

---

[27] Cf. George D. Spindler, "The Character Structure of Anthropology," in George D. Spindler, ed., *Education and Culture: Anthropological Approaches*, Holt, Rinehart and Winston, New York, 1963, pp. 12–13.
[28] E.g. by Jules Henry, George D. Spindler, Dorothy Lee, and Ruth Landes.
[29] Theodore Brameld, *Cultural Foundations of Education*, Harper and Row, New York, 1957.
[30] Spindler, *op. cit.*, p. 11.

of the assumptions that anthropologists bring to education and the assumptions that educational practices reflect.[31] For example most anthropologists working in education assume that the school is the most desirable form of educational institution—an acceptable enough assumption. But then they proceed as if it were an incontrovertible fact. Is the school *really* a "cultural good"? And how do we know unless we have a scheme of values to guide us? A set of experiments that assumed that schools were less effective than other media of education would clash with most of the data now gathered in educational anthropology. Apparently there are value orientations in anthropology that markedly affect its relation to education. It therefore becomes the responsibility of educators not only to explore these values, but also to order them and relate them to educational thought and practice as a whole.

---

[31] An example of an analysis of one such assumption is Philip J. Foster, "Status, Power, and Education in a Traditional Community," *The School Review* (Summer, 1964), pp. 158–182, esp. p. 180.

2

Theories of Culture

THREE VIEWS OF CULTURE

If we are to apply the findings of anthropology to education, we must first ask ourselves a fundamental question: What sort of entity is culture? To put the question a little differently: What kind of reality does culture possess?

This question has been answered in three ways. According to the *superorganic* view, culture is a super-reality that exists over and beyond its individual carriers and makes its own laws. In the *conceptualist* view, culture is not an entity at all but rather a concept used by anthropologists to unify an array of otherwise separate facts. In the *realist* view, culture is both a concept and an empirical entity. It is a concept because it is the fundamental construct of the science of anthropology. It is an empirical entity because this concept denotes the way in which certain phenomena actually are organized.[1] All three points of view will be elucidated, because they bear upon two broad questions in education: (1)

---

[1] I have chosen these three conceptions of culture because they are the most relevant to the study of education. From a purely anthropological point of view the most appropriate triad would consist of the evolutionary, the historical, and the functional approaches to the study of culture. Let me remind the reader not to confuse the theory, held by certain anthropologists, that culture is *super*organic or a super-reality with the universally accepted fact that culture is *supra*organic—that is, not bound by biological laws.

Should the school seek primarily to influence the culture's development, or should it inculcate the culture's heritage? (2) Should the child learn this heritage as his teachers present it, or should he explore it on his own initiative, creating his personal picture of the culture?

The Superorganic View of Culture

The essence of the superorganic view is that culture is a reality *sui generis* and, therefore, must be explained in terms of its own laws. Although it is true that certain factors—technology and economics, for instance—may be the main sources of cultural growth, it does not follow that culture can be reduced to these factors. Culture is no more explained in terms of its sources than a molecule is understood in terms of its atoms; the sources explain how the culture came to be, not what it is. Culture, in short, is more than the result of social or economic forces; it is the reality that makes them possible.

No one has presented the superorganic view more effectively than its originator, Emile Durkheim. Culture, he said, consists of "social facts" and "collective representations," which are ways of thinking, acting, and feeling independent of and external to the individual. These ways of behaving exercise a power of coercion over the individual, in that he is penalized, either legally or morally, for not abiding by them. Social facts cannot be explained psychologically but only by means of other social facts. Thus, an idea or sentiment may first be voiced by a particular person, but it becomes a social fact only through intercourse with the ideas and feelings of others. (*Hamlet,* for example, is a social fact that cannot be attributed solely to the genius of William Shakespeare, since it was written in the English language, which was the joint product of countless persons before him. It also drew copiously on the ideas of the time and, moreover, had to be seen, heard, and read by other people in order to become a work of art at all.)

According to Durkheim, culture—here understood as the totality of social facts—is both immanent and transcendent. On the one hand, it works within individuals, leading them to behave in certain ways; on the other, it exists outside them in collective representations to which they must conform. Culture, he declared, is a "collective consciousness . . . a psychic being that has its own particular way of thought, feeling, and action different from that peculiar to the individuals who compose it." [2] Like Hegel, Durkheim believed that what is best in a man comes to him from his culture and is, in fact, his culture operating within him. Thus, a man fulfills himself to the extent that he becomes involved in his culture and makes its aspirations his own. Conversely, the more self-centered a man, the more limited his personality becomes and the more prone he is to suicide.[3]

Among English-speaking anthropologists, the superorganic view has been expounded by Bronislaw Malinowski and by A. L. Kroeber, who invented the term "superorganic" but has since moved closer to the conceptualist position.[4] Today its leading exponent is Leslie A. White.[5]

In the superorganic view, human behavior is culturally determined. Granted that the individual makes culture possible (for, to exist at all, culture must have human "carriers"), it no more follows that the individual causes his own behavior than that the actors of a play (without whom the play would be merely a script) decide what they will perform. Culture controls the lives of men as surely as the play controls the words and deeds of the actors.[6] The individual, says White, is essentially an organization of cultural forces and elements that have "impinged upon him

---

[2] Emile Durkheim, *Moral Education: A Study in the Theory and Application of the Study of Education*, Free Press of Glencoe, New York, 1961, p. 65. (However, commentators have failed to agree whether Durkheim meant this statement literally or whether in this and similar passages he was speaking metaphorically in order to emphasize the culture's independence of its individual members.)

[3] *Ibid.*, pp. 67–68.

[4] A. L. Kroeber, "The Superorganic," *American Anthropologist*, XIX (1917), 163–213.

[5] Leslie A. White, *The Science of Culture: A Study of Man and Civilization*, Farrar, Straus, New York, 1949.

[6] One can believe that culture determines the lives of individuals without necessarily holding the superorganic view that culture determines itself. According to Marx and Hegel, for instance, the individual is shaped by his culture but culture, in turn, is propelled by forces more powerful still—economic in the Marxist view, spiritual in the Hegelian.

from the outside and which find their overt expression through him. So conceived, the individual is but the expression of a supra-biological tradition in somatic form." [7] Man can dominate certain aspects of the natural world precisely because he exists outside them, having evolved a mode of being, culture, that is no longer wholly subject to the laws of nature. Culture, however, he cannot control, since he himself is part of it.[8]

In this view, the growth of culture, being determined, can be predicted scientifically. But prediction does not entail control. What we predict will, if we predict accurately, come to pass in any case. The purpose of prediction is not to obstruct the course of culture but rather to enable us to adjust more rationally to the events that we foresee. In this sense, knowledge confers a measure of power, for it enables us to control, if not the cultural forces themselves, at least in some degree our adjustment to them. To some extent it also influences their future evolution, since our successful adaptation is itself a factor in the sequence of cultural events and, therefore, not without effect on the events that follow it.

The fact of cultural determinism, then, does not justify inaction. If our culture decides what we shall strive for and how, and whether or not we shall attain it, the decision to strive is still our own. The cultural determinist does not claim that all human effort is futile. Rather, he states that although what we do is determined by our culture, we ourselves must nevertheless decide to do it. If we are apathetic, it is our own fault, not our culture's.[9]

The Superorganic View and Education. The superorganic view

---

[7] White, *op. cit.*, pp. 167 and 183: "The individual does the thinking and feeling—by definition. But . . . *what* he thinks and feels is determined not by himself but by the sociocultural system into which the accident of birth has placed him."

[8] *Ibid.*, p. 350:

It is precisely in the realm of the external world that man's control is possible. He can harness the energies of rivers, fuels, and atoms because he, as one of the forces of nature, lies *outside* their respective systems and can therefore act upon them. But man, as an animal organism, as a species, lies *within* the man-culture system, and there he is the dependent, not the independent, variable; his behavior is merely the function of his culture, not its determinant.

[9] *Ibid.*, p. 303.

has three main implications for education. One is that education is a process by which culture controls men and shapes them to its own ends. According to Leslie White:

Education is a means employed by society in carrying on its own activities, in striving for its own objectives. Thus, during peacetime, society educates for peace, but when the nation is at war, it educates for war. . . . It is not people who control their culture through education; it is rather the other way round; education, formal and informal, is the process of bringing each new generation under the control of a system of culture.[10]

To be sure, educational policies are decided by individuals, yet the latter are merely the means through which the forces of culture attain their objectives. When educators choose, culture chooses through them.

Again, if culture determines the behavior of its members, the curriculum must be built on a forthright study of the state of culture now and to come. It must include whatever ideas, attitudes, and skills seem likely to make the individual the most effective bearer of the forces of his culture. Electives, for instance, must be carefully screened in order to insure that they relate directly to the basic curriculum. In particular, no child is properly educated if he has been allowed to study only those elements of his culture that arouse his interest. Rather, he must concentrate on those elements that the educational authorities, after carefully examining the needs of the culture, deem it necessary for him to know.

The superorganic view also implies close governmental control of education to insure that teachers implant in the young those ideas, attitudes, and skills necessary to cultural survival. It also implies greater centralization, for contemporary industrial culture tends to obliterate regional differences and, hence, to insist upon the same basic education for all. Greater centralization and state control in their turn tend to restrict (but not necessarily to eliminate) the private school.

Criticism of the Superorganic View. Although it has not lacked

---

[10] Leslie A. White, *The Science of Culture: A Study of Man and Civilization*, Grove, New York, 1955, pp. 345–346.

persuasive exponents, the superorganic theory of culture, with its distinct Hegelian affinities, has never been widely accepted by English-speaking anthropologists. It was opposed from the outset by Franz Boas and later by his empiricist successors, who maintained that culture is not self-moving but rather the creation of individuals living together. Culture, said Boas, is not a "mystic entity." [11]

The superorganic view may be criticized for divorcing culture and its forces from the human agents that make them possible.[12] Observing how pervasive is the pressure of culture on human behavior, theorists of the superorganic mistakenly conclude that culture must be an independent entity. Yet, in fact, all cultural pressures are exerted by men. Inflation, for example, is a cultural "force"; it is the result of an increase in the volume of money over the output of goods and services. But it is men who make money, goods, and services. Inflation, then, is not a process independent of men but a result of certain kinds of collective human behavior. Similarly, organized education is not an autonomous cultural force but rather an instrument created and controlled by men in order to achieve certain ends. To picture men in the grip of superhuman forces is to indulge in a metaphor; the truth is that they are subject to the consequences of their own mass actions. As David Bidney remarks:

Cultural fatalism as a philosophy of cultural evolution owes its plausibility to the divorce or abstraction of human achievements from the psychodynamic human agents and activities by which they are produced. Once human ideas, social institutions, and technical inventions are regarded as impersonal, superorganic entities and endowed with a force of persistence and development of their own, *as if* they were their own causal agents, then it seems logical to disregard their human creators or agents as the primary self-determining factor—a tendency which I have elsewhere designated as "the culturalistic fallacy." [13]

---

11 Franz Boas, *Anthropology and Modern Life*, Norton, New York, 1928, p. 234.
12 Clyde Kluckhohn and William H. Kelly, "The Concept of Culture," in Ralph Linton, ed., *The Science of Man in the World Crisis*, Columbia University Press, New York, 1945, p. 94.
13 David Bidney, "The Concept of Meta-Anthropology and Its Significance for Contemporary Anthropological Science," in F. S. C. Northrop, ed., *Ideological Differences and World Order: Studies in the Philosophy and Science of the World's Cultures*, Yale University Press, New Haven, 1949, p. 346.

One may also object that the individual, on the one hand, and culture conceived as superorganic, on the other, are incommensurable and, hence, cannot possibly interact.[14] For in what empirically ascertainable ways can a superorganic reality enter into a man's life and mold his behavior? The verifiable causes of this behavior are such factors as his psychophysical makeup, his past, material things, and other people. To reply that these are themselves intermediaries of culture is merely to shift the problem back a stage, for how does a superorganic culture make contact with these intermediaries?

But the main objection is that although culture determines much of the form and content of individual behavior, it does not determine behavior entirely.[15] Within certain bounds laid down by culture, I exercise genuine choice. Culture may prescribe the range of careers that I choose from, but it does not force me to elect one rather than another; it may offer me certain kinds of food, but, except on rare occasions, it does not dictate which I must eat; it may provide films rather than cockfights for entertainment, but it does not determine the particular film I decide to see, and it only partly shapes my judgment of the film. Culture, then, sets limits to my actions, but within those limits I am relatively free from its determinism. [16]

---

[14] Cf. Philip H. Bagby, "Culture and the Causes of Culture," *American Anthropologist*, LV, No. 4 (October 1953), 547–550.

[15] See A. F. C. Wallace, "Individual Difference and Cultural Uniformities," *American Sociological Review*, XVII (December 1952), 747. Wallace points out that a person with a problem will probably use *some* culturally recognized technique to solve it, but that his freedom of choice will vary "according to the number of systematic and random alternatives his culture affords for the solution of the problem, and the extent to which the given area of behavior is culturally standardized at all."

[16] Cf. Philip H. Bagby, *op. cit.*, 551:

"That men make choices, that they sometimes discover novel means of expression, novel solutions to long-standing problems seems to be an undeniable datum of experience, and free-will, in this sense, undeniably exists. But no one doubts that men's choices are always partly determined by the unalterable circumstances with which they are confronted and by their own predispositions towards particular ends. The scientific student of man . . . seeks to discover precisely how far they are determined. As a scientist, he must deal with the order, the regularities in his chosen field, and the irregularities, the novelty or originality of certain human actions, must always escape his net."

Indeed, the very fact that cultural norms are learned makes full cultural determinism impossible. Since no two people learn identically, each person, to a degree, interprets his culture uniquely. Granted that nearly every human experience has its cultural component, by what criteria do we decide that culture has determined an event rather than influenced it? Suppose that I send my child to a private school because I can afford it. True, culture is a necessary condition for my making this choice, because it is culture that provides the private school and the means by which I make my money. But a necessary condition is not equivalent to a determining factor. Suppose, too, that I choose a private school because I judge it to be the best kind of education available in my culture. Yet, this hardly presupposes that culture actually determines my decision. All that can be said is that culture is one of a number of factors influencing my choice. As Kluckhohn and Kelly have written:

"Culture determines" is a very inexact and elliptical way of speaking, justified perhaps in certain circumstances by the convenience of brevity. Inexact, however, it is, because no concrete phenomenon is ever completely and solely determined by culture. Sometimes, to be sure, culture may be the "strategic factor"—that is, the crucial element that determines that a different act tends to be differently carried out in one group than in another or that the act is somehow not what we would anticipate from a knowledge of the physical and biological forces operative. But "cultural determinism" in any simple or literal sense is as objectionable as any other class of unilateral determinism such as "geographic determinism" or "economic determinism." [17]

Undoubtedly, culture is *supra*organic in the sense that it outlives individuals and is largely responsible for molding human behavior. But it is not an independent entity, self-caused and self-directing. Why, then, has the theory of the *super*organic been so persuasive? The reason seems to be this: Having learned thoroughly the forms of conduct acceptable to his society, the individual performs them, in the main, unconsciously and with few conflicts with other individuals. Thus, he appears to be obeying patterns of behavior that exist independently of himself. In reality,

---

[17] Clyde Kluckhohn and William H. Kelly, "The Concept of Culture," in Ralph Linton, ed., *The Science of Man in the World Crisis,* Columbia University Press, New York, 1945, p. 94.

however, he is conforming to the habits in which he has been enculturated. Habits may condition men, but they are not independent of them.[18]

The Conceptualist View of Culture

Most American anthropologists hold what has been called the conceptualist view of culture. Culture, they say, is an anthropologist's *concept* or construct. What men observe is never culture as such but rather many forms of learned and shared behavior together with their material products. From these the notion of culture is abstracted. [19]

According to the conceptualist, all culture must finally be explained sociopsychologically. In Ralph Linton's words, "Culture . . . exists only in the minds of the individuals who compose a society. It derives all its qualities from their personalities and the interaction of those personalities." [20] It is not culture that causes cultural processes to happen but rather people themselves, influenced by what other people have done in the past. A cultural practice, such as shaking hands or drinking coffee, an artifact, like the airplane, a belief, such as monotheism, are not generated by superhuman forces; they are brought into being by the needs of men living together.

If the conceptualist reifies culture and its patterns, it is only for purposes of study and not because he believes that they are real entities. Nevertheless, conceptualists by no means agree on how far the individual can influence cultural processes. Some, like

---

[18] Cf. Melville J. Herskovits, *Cultural Anthropology*, Knopf, New York, 1955, p. 330.

[19] A. L. Kroeber and Clyde Kluckhohn, *Culture: A Critical Review of Concepts and Definitions*, Papers of the Peabody Museum of American Archaeology and Ethnology, Harvard University Press, XLVII, No. 1, 1952. Kluckhohn himself makes the same point more picturesquely: "Culture is like a map. Just as the map itself isn't the territory but the abstract representation of a particular area, so also a culture is an abstract description of trends toward uniformity in the words, deeds, and artifacts of a human group." *Mirror for Man: The Relation of Anthropology to Modern Life*, Whittlesey House, New York, 1949, p. 28.

[20] Ralph Linton, *The Study of Man*, Appleton-Century-Crofts, New York, 1936, p. 464.

Herskovits, [21] explain all cultural patterns ultimately in terms of individual behavior; others, like Kroeber, [22] a hesitant convert to the conceptualist position, maintain that it is much easier to explain them in terms of other culture patterns. Cultural events, says Kroeber, are patterned, but not in a way that is traceable to specific psychological or social causes.[23]

The Conceptualist View and Education. Since it treats culture as a quality of human behavior rather than as an entity in its own right, conceptualism accords with, but does not entail, the view that the child should learn the cultural heritage in keeping with his own interests. He should construct his picture of the culture in the light of his own experience, provided that he tests his learning against the learning of others and provided that he finally reaches an objective picture of the culture. Nevertheless, conceptualism lends no support to the subjectivist view that the child should learn solely as the spirit moves him. Culture as such may not be an absolute reality, but it comprises a great many patterns of behavior to which the individual must adjust in the same way that other people do. He must, therefore, learn these patterns and not merely whatever he likes.

Conceptualism is compatible with, but again does not entail, the principle that education can be an instrument of social re-

---

[21] Melville J. Herskovits, *Man and His Works,* Knopf, New York, 1948, p. 626.
[22] A. L. Kroeber, *The Nature of Culture,* University of Chicago Press, 1952, p. 112: "I would now say that culture was *primarily* intelligible in terms of itself, not *only* in terms of itself."
[23] Kroeber, *op. cit.,* p. 114 (Copyright 1952 University of Chicago.)
The efficient causes of cultural phenomena unquestionably are men: individual personalities who are in interpersonal and social relations. . . . But the manifestations of culture come characteristically in certain forms, patterns, or configurations, many of which are large, ramifying, and enduring. Now while persons undoubtedly make and produce these cultural forms, our knowledge of persons—and very largely also our knowledge of societies of persons—has failed conspicuously to explain the cultural *forms:* it has failed to derive specific cultural effects from specific psychic or social causes. . . . Such descriptions [in terms of "psychological and social concepts or mechanisms"] begin to mean something only when they are made on the cultural level—in terms of intercultural relations and of cultural values. . . . In other words, cultural forms or patterns gain in intelligibility as they are set in relation to other cultural patterns.

form. Doubtless, no conceptualist would expect as much of the school as does the social reconstructionist (pp. 87-89). Nevertheless, many conceptualists would agree that, although the school may not be able to change the culture, it can do much to create a climate of opinion conducive to change—a climate that is necessary if innovating individuals are to find imitators and so initiate new and permanent patterns. [24]

The Realist View of Culture

A few theoretical anthropologists, such as David Bidney and the historian Philip Bagby, maintain that culture is both a concept and a reality. Bagby argues that culture is an abstraction in the sense that, as a rule, neither it nor any of its constituent patterns can be observed in their entirety. How rarely, for instance, are all the members of a tribe present together so that the anthropologist can take in at a glance a single pattern of their culture. But he also points out that, although we never observe simultaneously all the movements of all the planets about the sun, we nevertheless accept the reality of the solar system. Why not, then, the reality of culture? [25] Culture as such, then, is a construct in the sense that in itself it is not an observable entity. But in another sense culture as such is real, for even if we cannot observe it in full all at once, it does not differ in this respect from other entities, such as the solar system, whose reality we do not question.

Bidney, too, postulates an actual culture from which the concept of culture is abstracted. [26] He states also that there is an abso-

---

[24] Kroeber's views, on the other hand, imply that the school is less likely to instigate changes in culture than it is to perpetuate the heritage of culture as it stands.

[25] Philip H. Bagby, *Culture and History*, Longmans, Green, London, 1958, pp. 91–92.

[26] David Bidney, "The Philosophical Presuppositions of Cultural Relativism and Cultural Absolutism," in Leo R. Ward, ed., *Ethics and the Social Sciences*, University of Notre Dame Press, 1959, pp. 52–53:

In my opinion, it is Kroeber and Kluckhohn who have confused the concept of culture which is indeed a logical construct, and the actual, existential culture which is a distinctive mode of actual, historic living in human society. Actual, existential culture is a precondition of the abstraction or logical construct in the mind of the anthropologist but there is more to culture than the abstractions of the anthropologist.

lute, "meta-cultural reality," which all cultures approximate but never attain. The latter represents the culture that, if it could be realized, would answer most completely the needs of human nature. No culture, then, is absolutely valid, but each reflects, however imperfectly, this ideal reality.[27]

Realists and conceptualists agree in rejecting full cultural determinism. Although past and present events limit what the members of a culture can do at any given moment, nevertheless, says Kluckhohn, cultures do not follow an inexorable logic of their own. There are times when a people can choose their own destiny. (Germany in 1933 and England in 1940 are cases in point.) [28]

Also, the immediate cause of social change is individual maladjustment. In times of widespread dissatisfaction a few creative individuals can initiate new culture patterns that are rapidly accepted by others. Social change thus has its origin in the strains and dissatisfactions felt by specific individuals. When personal insecurity is sufficiently intense and sufficiently widespread, new

---

[27] *Ibid.*, p. 71:

The absolute norm is real insofar as it is conceived as an ideal possibility whose validity is independent of its actual realization in a particular culture. Hence the ideal may serve as a goal of cultural endeavor which is radically different from the process, the going, whereby it is approximated. The moment this absolute norm is given expression within the content of a given culture, it becomes in part, falsified. That is why every attempt to identify the ideal with the actually existent is a delusion, a myth which sets up a false idol and hinders cultural progress. The ideal absolute is compatible with cultural freedom and diversity, since it does not dictate categorically the particular form which all historical cultures must assume, but serves only as a regulative norm and measure by which to evaluate cultural expressions.

[28] Clyde Kluckhohn, *Mirror for Man: The Relation of Anthropology to Modern Life*, Whittlesey House, New York, 1949, p. 260:

While choice is most often a flattering illusion, while antecedent and existent hard sense data usually shape our destinies, there are moments in the careers of nations, as well as in the careers of individuals, when opposing external forces are about equally balanced, and it is then that intangibles like "will" and "belief" throw the scales. Cultures are not altogether self-contained systems which inevitably follow out their own self-determined evolution. Sorokin and other prophets of doom fail to see that one of the factors which determines the next step in the evolution is precisely the dominant attitudes of people. And these are not completely determined by the existent culture.

patterns are germinated in a few creative individuals and gradually adopted by the whole society. [29]

The Realist View and Education. The realist view of culture is closer to those schools of educational thought that believe in adjusting the child to an objective reality, both natural and cultural, by inculcating certain knowledge, values, and skills that the culture has selected already. More emphatically than conceptualism realism implies an educational system that will train people to judge and to change their culture according to its own fundamental values. Many educational traditionalists want to achieve this end by educating the young in supposedly permanent truths and values, by means of which young people can tell what actual changes they should help, hinder, or initiate. Other traditional educators advocate a mainly scientific training, necessary for young people if they are to select those goals that the state of culture permits and if they are to use the laws of culture, as far as they are known, in order to realize such goals. Change, in other

---

[29] *Ibid.*, p. 255. Other conceptualists, such as Kroeber, although not denying a measure of personal freedom, emphasize more strongly the pressure that culture exerts on individuals. A. L. Kroeber, *The Nature of Culture*, *op. cit.*, pp. 132–133 (Copyright 1952 University of Chicago.)

The human beings who influence culture and make new culture are themselves molded; and they are molded through the intervention of other men who are culturalized and thus products of previous culture. So it is clear that, while human beings are always the immediate causes of cultural events, these human causes are themselves the result of antecedent cultural situations, having been fitted to the existing cultural forms which they encounter. There is thus a continuity of indirect causation from culture event to culture event through the medium of human intermediaries. These intermediaries are concerned, first of all, with relieving their own tensions and achieving their personal gratification; but in so doing they also transmit, and to some degree modify, the culture which they carry because they have been conditioned to it. In a sense, accordingly, a kind of cultural causality is operative. However, compared with the immediate efficient causality of men on culture, the causation of culture on culture is indirect, remote, and largely a functional relation of form to form. At any rate, as long as one's interest is in what happens in culture, it is the cultural antecedents that become significant. The human transmitters and carriers and modifiers are likely to average pretty much alike. As causes they tend to average uniform and constant, except so far as cultural exposure has differentiated them.

words, must be evolutionary, not revolutionary. It must be guided by the culture's fundamental assumptions.

CULTURE AS RELATIVE OR UNIVERSAL

If we are to apply the findings of anthropology to education, we must also ask ourselves whether the experience of any culture can ever be a model for other cultures. To put it another way, we must ask whether or not there are values and practices that all cultures hold or can hold in common. The idea that all cultures may have specific common features, as opposed to certain broad and formal similarities, is taken more seriously now than it was a generation ago, when cultural relativism reigned virtually supreme. For, although most nineteenth century anthropologists regarded the "psychic unity" of mankind almost as an article of faith, the great anthropological discovery of the early twentieth century was the sheer diversity of cultural practice. True, in 1923 Clark Wissler proposed his "universal culture patterns" (that is, patterns of behavior common to all cultures), but for many years he found few imitators.[30] Only recently has the universalist view won the support of a substantial minority.[31]

In any comparison of cultures the main problem is to devise categories of comparison that are broad enough to apply to all the cultures under review and yet sufficiently specific to indicate more than the most rough-and-ready likenesses. Extreme relativists deny that categories can be fashioned that are both accurate and universal.[32] Both schools of thought agree, however, that the categories now in general use, such as social organization, technology, art, and religion, are too permeated by Western assumptions to do justice to the materials gathered in the field. In many primitive tribes, for instance, it is difficult to find anything strictly comparable to the Western notion of government. As a rule, the

---

[30] Clark Wissler, *Man and Culture*, Crowell, New York, 1923.
[31] See Richard Kluckhohn, ed., *Culture and Behavior: The Collected Essays of Clyde Kluckhohn*, The Free Press of Glencoe, New York, 1962, pp. 266–267.
[32] The problem is discussed by Clyde Kluckhohn, "Universal Categories of Culture," in A. L. Kroeber, ed., *Anthropology Today*, University of Chicago Press, 1953, pp. 507–523.

processes that are most adequately comparable are those closest to human biology, such as the satisfaction of fundamental physical needs.

Cultural Relativism

The essence of cultural relativism is that every culture is unique and must, therefore, be analyzed in its own terms. Cross-cultural comparison may reveal similarities between certain cultures but no qualities necessarily common to all of them; hence, universal classification is extremely difficult, perhaps impossible. Cultural relativism also implies that human nature is relative to time and place. If it were not, all cultures would have features in common.

In America cultural relativism was formulated explicitly by Franz Boas and the empiricist school in order to refute the nineteenth-century belief in a single highroad of cultural evolution. According to Boas, each culture is unique because it is the product in part of chance and nonrecurrent historical circumstances. Later, Ruth Benedict maintained that each culture is a unique and legitimate expression of human potentialities; hence, there is no universal norm of cultural practice.[33] The functionalists, too, were relativists in their contention that an item of culture must be judged solely by what it contributes to the well-being of its own culture and not by standards drawn from other cultures. More recently, Kroeber has argued that no comprehensive categories can be fashioned accurately enough to apply to particular phenomena in all cultures, and that the so-called universal categories break down at the point of application. The categories of *magic* and *religion,* for instance, have yet to be satisfactorily distinguished, because the phenomena they are designed to cover intermingle.[34] More recently still, Herskovits has maintained that universal categories are formal only, not substantive. They denote nothing that is at once specific and universal, since their content varies too much from one culture to another. The universals they designate are not actual patterns in the cultures themselves but

---

[33] Ruth Benedict, *Patterns of Culture,* Houghton Mifflin, Boston, 1934, p. 278: "[All cultures are] . . . the coexisting and equally valid patterns of life which mankind has carved for itself from the raw materials of existence."
[34] A. L. Kroeber, *The Nature of Culture,* University of Chicago Press, 1952.

constructs framed by the anthropologist as an aid in investigation and comparison.[35]

The virtue of the cultural relativist is that he eschews ethnocentrism. Abandoning, so far as he can, the mentality of his own culture and assuming that of the culture he is studying, he seeks to assess each phenomenon solely in terms of its significance for its own culture. For example, when he investigates the cultures of primitive tribes he treats the phenomenon of spirit possession as an important cultural experience rather than as the psychopathological seizure that most Westerners consider it to be. The weakness in cultural relativism, at any rate in its pure form, is that it inhibits the theoretical potential of anthropology by limiting judgments to single cultures.[36] Hitherto, the further a science has extended its theory, the better it has been able to explain the facts that it studies. Hence, anthropologists should be careful not to curtail unnecessarily their powers of generalization.

Cultural relativism is also a form of moral relativism, for it implies that moral values are valid only for the culture that holds them. It implies, for example, that we have no right to condemn apparent cruelties in the customs of other peoples, because to do so is to extend our own values beyond the only context in which they are legitimate.[37] The great merit in this kind of moral relativism is that it makes us tolerant of other cultures and unwilling

[35] Herskovits mentions the universals of technology, economy, family or broader kinship structure, political order, religion or philosophy, means of esthetic satisfaction, language, and ethics. See his *Cultural Anthropology,* Knopf, New York, 1955, pp. 307, 348–366.
[36] See M. Brewster Smith, "Anthropology and Psychology," in John Gillin, ed., *For a Science of Social Man,* Macmillan, New York, 1954, p. 46. Smith maintains that by definition all phenomena are unique and that one may seek to capture this uniqueness. Yet, he writes:

But one may also legitimately seek to abstract from phenomena analytical elements that can then be lawfully related. The lesson of the history of science is that this detour away from the compelling force of concrete reality greatly increases our powers of understanding it and coping with it in the longer run. Quite apart from the general question of the definition of science, however, it is clear that the psychologists, sociologists, and anthropologists who are groping toward a more comprehensive behavioral science are committed to pushing the latter sort of program as far as it can be extended.

[37] One can, of course, be a moral relativist without explicitly being a cultural

to settle their affairs in the name of our own values. Thus, Herskovits maintains that we should observe the moral code of our own culture while respecting the right of other people to observe the moral codes of theirs. If we hesitate to adopt this attitude, it is because of the moral absolutism in which we were reared.[38]

Yet cultural relativism also creates a moral problem of its own. Must we accept any custom as justified, no matter how abhorrent to us, as long as it forms an integral part of another culture? Have we no right to condemn genocide, cannibalism, slavery, and physical torture merely because they are practiced by other peoples? Even professed relativisits have been known to criticize practices that, in theory, they should have tolerated.[39] Again, suppose that a liberal minority within a culture condemns one of the culture's practices, such as racial segregation. What attitude are members of other cultures to adopt? Are they really to observe the strict letter of cultural relativism and accept the practice as justified within that culture, simply because they are outsiders? Moreover, how are we to judge such practices as public executions which some cultures have already repudiated? Must we accept such a practice as justified, even though in a number of years the culture itself may reject it?

Let me mention two other objections. First, by making the particular culture the ultimate frame of moral reference, the relativist implies that only individuals can be maladjusted, not cultures. As Erich Fromm has pointed out, the relativist cannot admit logically that a culture may distort the development of its members, because he denies that there are any criteria for the judgment of cultures.[40] Second, as David Bidney has shown, relativism

---

relativist. David Hume, for instance, believed moral judgments to be subjective, whereas the cultural relativist considers them to be intersubjective yet relative to the culture in which they are made. See David Bidney, "The Philosophical Presuppositions of Cultural Relativism and Cultural Absolutism" in Leo R. Ward, ed., *Ethics and the Social Sciences*, University of Notre Dame Press, 1959, p. 59.

[38] Melville Herskovits, *Man and His Works*, Knopf, New York, 1948, pp. 77–78.

[39] See Bronislaw Malinowski's denunciations of totalitarianism in his *Freedom and Civilization*, Allen and Unwin, London, 1947.

[40] Erich Fromm, *The Sane Society*, Routledge and Kegan Paul, London, 1956, pp. 12–13.

makes it impossible for us to improve our own culture by adopting other cultures' values that we might believe to be superior, because relativism makes it nonsensical to regard such values as superior at all.[41]

We may conclude that cultural relativism is justified as a rule of procedure for the investigation of particular cultures but that as a fundamental principle guiding anthropological theory it is highly vulnerable. The anthropologist is surely right to accept the customs of the culture that he is studying in order to understand the culture more fully from within. But the matter does not rest there. Unless the anthropologist generalizes from one culture to another, his science must necessarily remain at the stage of classification. Moreover, unless he does so, he cannot judge the adequacy of a given culture to human needs and aspirations. He cannot assess whether it frees or fetters the powers of man. Granted, many anthropologists prefer not to pass judgment, but others must. No branch of knowledge as broad as anthropology should evade its responsibility to appraise the human condition.[42]

Cultural Relativism and Education. If, as the relativist holds, each culture is unique, then each has its own needs that education must satisfy, and no one form of education is universally appropriate.[43]

Again, if, as the relativist also holds, the mature man is a product more of his culture than of anything called human nature, it follows that there is no single education suitable to man *per se* but only a range of educational systems appropriate to men of different cultures.[44]

41 David Bidney, "The Concept of Value in Modern Anthropology," in Sol Tax, ed., *Anthropology Today: Selections,* Phoenix Books, University of Chicago Press, 1962, pp. 444–445.
42 For a similar view see Paul F. Schmidt, "Some Criticisms of Cultural Relativism," *The Journal of Philosophy,* LII, No. 25 (December 8, 1955), 790–791.
43 Cf. Emile Durkheim, *Education and Society,* Free Press of Glencoe, New York, 1956, p. 64; and Ruth Benedict, "Transmitting Our Democratic Heritage in the Schools," in Blaine E. Mercer and Edwin R. Carr, eds., *Education and the Social Order,* Rinehart, New York, 1957, p. 214.
44 In Durkheim's words, "The man whom education should realize in us is not the man such as nature has made him, but as the society wishes him to be; and it wishes him such as its internal economy calls for. What proves

The progressive educator—that is, one who supports the educational movement known as "progressivism"—is a cultural relativist.[45] He believes, for example, that human nature, so far as it can be schooled, is the product of its own time and place. As Sidney Hook has said:

What is apparent is that those aspects of human nature which appear constant are a set of unconscious processes that are a condition of life. Although these are taken note of in any sensible educational program, they are far from the center of educational concern, which is understanding the dominant cultural problems of the present in relation to the past out of which they have grown, and to the future, whose shape depends in part upon that understanding. Whether men remain the same or different, in the sense in which the question is educationally significant, depends upon whether they choose to retain or transform their culture.[46]

Denying, as they do, that there is a universal human nature or a universal ideal of culture, cultural relativists generally draw our attention to the capacity of cultures for change. American anthropology, which is mainly relativist, stresses the innate dynamism of cultures. The progressive educator, too, declares that nothing in the nature of reality, knowledge, or value is inherently permanent. Education not only varies from one culture to another but may transform itself within the history of a single culture. The prime virtues, then, of any educational system, especially of those that must meet the unprecedented rate of change in modern industrial societies, are flexibility and willingness to experiment. The progressive also rejects any attempt to create a permanent hierarchy of studies. He argues not only that the worth

---

this is the manner in which our conception of man has varied from one society to another." *Education and Society,* Free Press of Glencoe, New York, 1956, p. 122.

[45] Progressivism is an educational theory that claims to base itself, among other things, on a philosophy of pragmatism. It maintains that the child should acquire knowledge "actively" by solving problems that genuinely concern him, and that the school should come to terms with the social issues of its time, especially by practicing democracy in the classroom. For further information on progressivism and other contemporary educational thories—perennialism, essentialism, and reconstructionism—see my *Introduction to the Philosophy of Education,* Wiley, New York, 1964.

[46] Sidney Hook, *Education for Modern Man: A New Perspective,* Knopf, New York, 1963, p. 76.

of a school subject is, in part, a function of its capacity to enhance the life of the individual student but also that time itself, which makes one subject particularly relevant now, may replace it shortly with another.

An emphasis on the mutability of cultures may lead to the belief that education itself can initiate changes in culture and even, perhaps, direct the course of culture. If culture is plastic, then education is not wholly bound by tradition but may be reasonably free to shape anew the coming generation. Thus, the progressive declares that the school should pave the way for rational change by cultivating in its pupils a critical and independent cast of mind. If people are educated to think experimentally, he says, they are unlikely to cling to outmoded patterns of thought and action, and they will be disposed to support or initiate new ones beneficial to society as a whole. Theodore Brameld's reconstructionism, less relativist than progressivism, is more ambitious in its social aims.[47] Brameld accuses progressivism of a relativism so sterile that it refuses to consider any long-term social goals whatever. As an alternative Brameld himself has drawn up a blueprint of the good society—a blueprint, he believes, that should be presented in the schools to the coming generation so that, as adults, they will legislate it into effect. Although Brameld provokes the obvious relativist retort that his "paper utopia" will soon be out of date, he replies that his plan is flexible enough to allow modification without compromising its essential character.

Cultural Universalism

Although he concedes the fact of cultural diversity, the universalist nevertheless maintains that, since (as he believes) human nature in its essential form is universal, culture must be so too.[48] This uni-

---

[47] Reconstructionism is the theory that the chief purpose of education is to "reconstruct" society to meet the cultural crisis of our time. It has been expounded by Theodore Brameld chiefly in three books: *Patterns of Educational Philosophy*, World, Yonkers, New York, 1950; *Philosophies of Education in Cultural Perspective*, Dryden, New York, 1955; and *Toward a Reconstructed Philosophy of Education*, Dryden, New York, 1956.
[48] See Clyde Kluckhohn, "Universal Categories of Culture," in A. L. Kroeber, ed., *Anthropology Today*, University of Chicago Press, 1953, p. 520: "The

versal human nature may not explain the diversity of cultures, but it does account for the features that they have in common. It also implies, as Fromm points out, that it is not enough for us to consider only the individual's adjustment to his culture; we must also examine the culture's adjustment to the objective needs of man. Mental health, in other words, may be as much the product of the right kind of culture as of the right kind of individual.[49]

In important respects the human lot is universal. Certain facts of biology and psychology together with certain circumstances of social life are common to all men everywhere and, therefore, demand certain forms of cultural expression. All cultures must come to terms with the universal necessities of human living. Kluckhohn summarizes these necessities:

All cultures constitute so many distinct answers to essentially the same questions posed by human biology and by the generalities of the human situation. . . . Every society's patterns for living must provide approved and sanctioned ways for dealing with such universal circumstances as the existence of two sexes; the helplessness of infants, the need for satisfaction of the elementary biological requirements such as food, warmth, and sex; the presence of individuals of different ages and of differing physical and other capacities. The basic similarities in human biology the world over are vastly more massive than the variations. Equally, there are certain necessities in social life for this kind of animal, regardless of where that life is carried on or in what culture. Cooperation to acquire subsistence and for other ends requires a certain minimum of reciprocal behavior, of a standard system of communication, and, indeed, of mutually accepted values. The facts of human biology and of human gregariousness supply, therefore, certain invariant points of reference from which cross–cultural comparisons can start without begging questions that are themselves at issue.[50]

What are some of the universal characteristics of culture? Robert Redfield cites the following: All cultures set moral limits to vio-

---

inescapable fact of cultural relativism does not justify the conclusion that cultures are in all respects utterly disparate monads and hence strictly noncomparable entities."
[49] Erich Fromm, *The Sane Society*, Routledge and Kegan Paul, London, 1956, p. 72.
[50] Clyde Kluckhohn, "Universal Categories of Culture," in A. L. Kroeber, ed., *Anthropology Today*, University of Chicago Press, 1953, pp. 520–521. (Copyright 1953 University of Chicago.)

lence. All cultivate a sense of loyalty. All have certain ways, such as hunting, fishing, or manufacturing, of winning a livelihood. All have codified family systems, which generate such qualities as warmth of feeling for others and a sense of mutual dependence. All have some conception of the universe and man's place in it. All have a moral code. All are creative beyond the needs of mere survival; for instance, all indulge to no purely practical end in myths, legends, artifacts, songs, dances, and other modes of esthetic expression.[51] Other frequently cited universals are: language, a theory of the culture's origins, a set of attitudes toward such fundamental problems as death, and some form of law and order or social organization.[52]

George P. Murdock has alphabetized a surprisingly large number of elements that he believes to be common to all known cultures, beginning with age-grading, athletics, bodily adornment, calendars, and cleanliness training, and ending with religious rituals, resident rules, sexual restrictions, soul concepts, status differentiation, surgery, tool making, trade, visiting, weaning, and weather control.[53]

On such similar foundations each society raises its distinctive superstructure of culture. Thus, a single human need or interest may generate a multitude of cultural expressions. Some cultures forbid sexual intercourse before marriage; others, like the Polynesian, regard it as normal; some, like our own, prefer lifelong monogamy; others, serial monogamy; some, polygamy; others still,

---

51 Robert Redfield, "Anthropology's Contribution to the Understanding of Man," *Anthropological Quarterly*, Redfield Commemorative Issue, XXXII, No. 1 (January 1959), 13–18.

52 Clark Wissler maintains that each culture displays a "universal culture pattern" of speech (languages, writing systems, etc.), material habits (food habits, shelter, transportation and travel, dress, utensils and tools, weapons, occupations and industries), art (carving, painting, drawing, music, etc.), mythology and scientific knowledge, religious practices (ritualistic practices, treatment of the sick and the dead), family and social systems (forms of marriage, methods of reckoning relationship, inheritance, social control, sports and games), property (property real and personal, standards of value and exchange, trade), government (political forms, judicial and legal procedures), and war. See his *Man and Culture*, Crowell, New York, 1923, pp. 50–77.

53 George P. Murdock, "The Common Denominator of Cultures," in Ralph Linton, ed., *The Science of Man in the World Crisis*, Columbia University Press, New York, 1945, pp. 124 ff.

polyandry.[54] The human drive is the same; each culture meets it in its own way.[55]

Cultural universalism implies moral universalism. All cultures, in this view, recognize certain common values that are appropriate to the needs of human nature. In David Bidney's words:

Thus, for all cultures, the perpetuation of the society takes precedence over the life of the individual and hence no society tolerates treason, murder, rape, or incest. All societies recognize mutual rights and duties in marriage and condemn acts which threaten family solidarity. Similarly all societies give recognition to personal property and provide some techniques for the distribution of economic surplus to the needy.[56]

These values do not merely represent formal concepts devised by anthropologists but are actual attitudes common to all cultures.[57]

The universalist also argues that, even if, in fact, men did acknowledge different values, it would not follow that they *should* do so.[58] Bidney, for example, maintains that whether or not man observes it, an objective moral order is enjoined on him as a ra-

---

[54] Of course, as some commentators observe, if the rate of divorce and separation continues to rise, monogamy in the West soon will be as much serial as lifelong.

[55] Melford E. Spiro, "Social Systems, Personality, and Functional Analysis," in Bert Kaplan, ed., *Studying Personality Cross–Culturally*, Row, Peterson, Evanston, Illinois, 1961, p. 104: "Although cultural goals are parochial, most human drives—because of their rootedness in a common biology and in common conditions of social life—are universal. Hence . . . the quite diverse goals of different societies, as well as the roles which are instrumental for their attainment, are functionally equivalent; they serve to gratify the same drives."

[56] David Bidney, "The Philosophical Presuppositions of Cultural Relativism and Cultural Absolutism," in Leo R. Ward, ed., *Ethics and the Social Sciences,* University of Notre Dame Press, 1959, pp. 62–63.

[57] *Ibid.,* p. 63:

There are concrete, cultural universals because there are universal needs, biological, derived, and integrative, common to all societies. These cultural universals, comprising institutions and values, are not merely abstract categories but actual, regulative modes of conduct, common to all cultures. Such transcultural values implicit in all cultures may be called absolutes as well as universals since they do not vary from culture to culture.

[58] See Paul F. Schmidt, "Some Criticisms of Cultural Relativism," *The Journal of Philosophy,* LII, No. 25 (December 28, 1955), 783.

tional being.[59] In other words, all men as rational beings share the same nature, which demands the same values for its expression. If they follow different values, it is not because their natures are fundamentally different but because they have not fulfilled the nature that they have in common.

Cultural Universalism and Education. According to the educational theory of *perennialism,* human nature is universal.[60] Man's essence consists in the end for which he exists, which is to be rational. However much men may seem to differ from one culture to another, this end remains the same. Therefore, all forms of education under all conditions have one abiding ideal, whether or not it is acknowledged—to cultivate the rational faculty and so "to improve man as man." [61] Nevertheless, since the forces that impinge on human nature are constantly changing, the *means* used to attain this ideal will vary from culture to culture. Moreover, as our knowledge of human nature increases, the more so as it is studied scientifically, the means also will improve. Thus, American education is benefiting from the insights of psychology as well as from new understandings of the nonrational aspects of the child's nature. But such variations in the means of education do not change its fundamental purpose. This purpose holds good even if it goes unrecognized, for it springs from what men essentially are and always will be—rational beings.

The perennialist also maintains that education should concentrate on those qualities, preeminently rational, that all men have in common rather than on the felt needs and interests of the individual child. Hutchins has said, "I do not deny the fact of individual differences; I deny that it is the most important fact about men or the one on which an educational system should be erected. . . . Now, if ever, we need an education that is designed to bring

---

[59] Bidney, *op. cit.,* pp. 64–65, and "The Concept of Value in Modern Anthropology," in Sol Tax, ed., *Anthropology Today: Selections,* Phoenix Books, University of Chicago Press, 1962, p. 446.

[60] Perennialism is the theory that education should be based on changeless, universal principles and that its prime end should be the cultivation of the intellect. Its best-known exponents are Mortimer J. Adler and Robert M. Hutchins.

[61] Robert M. Hutchins, *The Conflict in Education in a Democratic Society,* Harper, New York, 1953, p. 68.

out our common humanity rather than to indulge our individuality." [62]

Two objections to cultural universalism need to be stated at this point. One is that the universalist may distort the particular facts of different cultures in order to fit them into his all too comprehensive categories. The other is that he runs the risk of applying the norms of his own culture to the human race as a whole. He may, for instance, take for a universal model an educational system that is appropriate only to a certain stage in the development of a particular Western culture. All perennialists, for example, want to teach certain moral and spiritual values, which they maintain to be absolute and universal. Based on the Judeo-Christian heritage, these values constitute the norms of ethical behavior for most educational systems of the Western world. What would the Western universalist do if his Eastern colleague insisted on transferring oriental ethical norms to the West in the name of universalizing them?

In this chapter I have considered two important and related questions in anthropology: (1) What is the nature of culture? (2) Is culture relative or universal? I have shown that different educational theories influencing the practice of our schools today presuppose different answers to these questions. In order fully to understand these theories, one must grasp the anthropological assumptions that lie behind them.

---

[62] *Ibid.*, pp. 89–90.

3
Man, Culture, Personality

MAN AS CREATURE AND CREATOR OF CULTURE

Culture is at once the creation of man and the condition of human living. Man creates culture but culture, in turn, makes man. If you doubt this, look at a young child. Although wholly dependent on others, the infant is unrestrained in his emotions, utterly unsocialized, and incapable of sharing his possessions. Anticipating no future, he seeks instant and constant satisfaction. Yet, he becomes an adult with ordered desires and aversions, able to take part in the life of a complex society.

What makes this possible is *enculturation* or the *internalization* of culture, a process by which the person absorbs the modes of thought, action, and feeling that constitute his culture.[1] Children

---

[1] Enculturation is therefore a more inclusive term than socialization, which refers to the process by which a person becomes a member of society—i.e. learns to behave in such a way as to acquire statuses and roles in society. See Felix M. Keesing, *Cultural Anthropology: The Science of Custom*, Rinehart, New York, 1958, p. 35. For a definition of enculturation, see Melville J. Herskovits, *Cultural Anthropology*, Knopf, New York, 1955, p. 326: "This is in essence a process of conscious or unconscious conditioning, exercised within the limits sanctioned by a given body of custom. From this process not only is all adjustment to social living achieved, but also all those satisfactions, themselves a part of social experience, that derive from individual expression rather than association with others in the group."

brought up by animals behave like animals, although, if recaptured young enough, their human potentialities may still be realized. It is only enculturation that transforms the limited, untaught animal, *homo sapiens*, into a recognizable human being.[2]

During childhood and youth, enculturation stabilizes culture because it builds socially acceptable habits into the growing personality. In adulthood it often promotes change, since many forms of behavior that require enculturation on the part of the adult probably are new not only to him but also to the culture. As Herskovits has pointed out:

> The difference between the nature of the enculturative experience in the early years of life and later is that the range of conscious acceptance or rejection by an individual continuously increases as he grows older. By the time he has reached maturity, a man or woman has been so conditioned that he moves easily within the limits of accepted behavior set by his group. Thereafter, new forms of behavior presented to him are in the main those involved in culture change—new inventions or discoveries, new ideas diffused from outside his society about which, as an individual, he has to "make up his mind" and thus play his role in reorienting his culture. . . . The enculturation of the individual during the early years of his life is the prime mechanism making for cultural stability, while the process, as it is operative on more mature folk, is highly important in inducing change.[3]

Nevertheless, this point can be overstated, for much adult enculturation is also the result of movement into another area of existing culture, owing, perhaps, to a change in home, status (such as marriage), class, or occupation.

It is clear that, the more thoroughly the child is enculturated and the deeper the habits of culture are driven in, the more rigid the adult is likely to be. Hence, the importance, especially in a swiftly changing and democratic society, of training an inde-

---

2 Cf. Richard Church, *Language and the Discovery of Reality*, Random House, New York, 1961, p. 137: "A human being can be a human being only because other people have taught him, directly and indirectly, explicitly and implicitly, how to be human and what the important characteristics of the world, human and nonhuman, are that he is going to have to live with."

3 Melville J. Herskovits, *Man and His Works*, Knopf, New York, 1956, p. 40. (italics deleted)

pendent and critical judgment from the earliest years if we want to foster open-mindedness and flexibility.[4]

Nature has fully equipped the animal for life; its upbringing merely develops more quickly the instincts that it possesses already. But the aptitudes required for life among men are too complex to be transmitted genetically and must, therefore, be learned afresh by each generation. Man has, it is true, certain innate dispositions—to self-preservation, for instance, and to the satisfaction of hunger and sex—but they are general and vague, and he must be taught to consummate them satisfactorily.[5]

Culture, then, pervades our waking lives. It even enters our sleep in the posture that we adopt and in the content of our dreams.[6] Not even the infant of a few weeks responds to a situation entirely afresh. Few human experiences can be explained wholly in terms of the individual's biology or his history or the

---

[4] Franz Boas, *Anthropology and Modern Life*, Norton, New York, 1928, p. 181:

> The firmer the habits that are instilled into the child and the less they are subject to reasoning, the stronger is their emotional appeal. If we wish to educate children to unreasoned mass action, we must cultivate set habits of action and thought. If we wish to educate them to intellectual and emotional freedom, care must be taken that no unreasoned action takes such habitual hold on them that a serious struggle is involved in the attempt to cast it off.

[5] As Durkheim has said:

> These are drives in a given direction; but the means by which these drives are expressed vary from one individual to another, from one occasion to another. A large area remains reserved, then, for trial and error, for personal reflections and, consequently, for the effect of causes which can make their influence felt only after birth. Now, education is one of these causes.

Emile Durkheim, *Education and Society*, Free Press of Glencoe, New York, 1956, p. 83.

[6] A modern American would find it hard to sleep on a mat spread on the ground or in a slatted hammock, yet people accustomed to a mat or hammock find springs and mattresses just as uncomfortable. When European and American missionaries installed Western style beds in their first hospitals in the interior of Central Africa, they found that many patients, disconcerted by the high beds with their soft mattresses and elastic springs, preferred to sleep on the floor beneath them. Ina Corrine Brown, *Understanding Other Cultures*, Prentice-Hall, Englewood Cliffs, New Jersey, 1963, p. 81.

facts of his particular situation; rather, each experience of his life brings into play some part of what he has acquired from his culture.

Culture shapes us intellectually, emotionally, and even physically. It conditions such physical traits as gestures, facial expressions, and ways of walking, sitting, eating, and sleeping. When not standing or moving about, Western adults generally sit on chairs, benches, or couches. We would find it highly uncomfortable to squat on the floor or sit cross-legged for any length of time, or to sit either with our legs straight out in front or on a low stool with no backrest. Nor could we relax by standing on one leg and resting the other foot on our knee, as is the practice among some of the Nilotic tribes in Africa. Yet, in India village women perform their household chores sitting or squatting on the floor, and until recently Japanese women worked and visited either kneeling or sitting on their heels.

Culture prescribes what emotions may be expressed and by whom, where, and how. In America today, men are allowed to be more aggressive than women, and in sexual relations they are expected to take the initiative. Hostility may not be indulged publicly except in war or sport or very unusual circumstances. On the other hand, the drive to succeed and to make money may be expressed in public virtually without restraint.[7]

Different cultures—and the same culture at different periods—may estimate equivalent emotions very differently.[8] Contrast the free and easy manners of the modern American with the extreme self-restraint of the Menomini Indian or with the puritanism of the early New Englander. Culture decrees, too, how feelings are to be expressed. All people laugh and cry, but different cultures find different modes of expression for the subtler shades of anger, grief, joy, shame, and other feelings.

Culture defines how we think about the world and how we perceive it. Each culture flings the network of its symbols over reality,

---

[7] Cf. Jules Henry, *Culture Against Man*, Random House, New York, 1963, p. 30.
[8] Cf. George D. Spindler, "Personality, Sociocultural System, and Education among the Menomini" in George D. Spindler, ed., *Education and Culture: Anthropological Approaches*, Holt, Rinehart and Winston, New York, 1963, pp. 356–361.

so that each of us apprehends this reality through the symbols his culture affords him. Indeed, reality only exists for us insofar as culture has made it accessible. As Dorothy Lee has said, "Culture is a symbolic system which transforms the physical reality, what is *there*, into experienced reality." [9]

Consider something as familiar as a tree. Modern man regards a tree as an object that he can use for decoration, agriculture, or reforestation. To the Dakota Black Elm Indians, on the other hand, trees were persons with the same right to the land as himself, "standing peoples, in whom the winged ones built their lodges and reared their families." Consider something as fundamental as our interpretation of reality. Modern man believes that objects are located separately in space and time and that events occur discretely in causal sequences. For the Trobriand Islander, however, reality is a whole with no distinction of space and time and no separateness of things. In his view a man does not walk *from* one point *to* another but is always *at* a point. All events form patterns and all patterns merge into a single whole. Thus, whereas for us a thing is meaningful when it can be causally explained, for him it is only significant when it can be accommodated to an established pattern.[10]

No matter how small the culture, no member is wholly cognizant of its heritage or wholly competent in all its activities. All cultures admit some specialization. All, for instance, divide the functions of labor between men and women. A large society especially, stratified according to class and function, narrows considerably the area of individual participation, separating the spheres of priests, warriors, traders, administrators, and others. Contemporary industrial societies, with their great size and centralization, their extreme specialization, and their vast accumulation of knowledge, curtail still further the range of individual knowledge and participation. On the other hand, they seek increasingly to amplify the opportunities of the mass of people. Thus, they use education both to increase the division of function (by training for the manifold occupations that a changing technology ceaselessly creates) and also to open the way for a fuller life.

[9] Dorothy Lee, *Freedom and Culture*, Prentice-Hall, Englewood Cliffs, New Jersey, 1959, p. 1.
[10] *Ibid.*, pp. 1, 105–120.

The Transmission of Culture

Culture is transmitted through the communication of symbols. Man, as Ernst Cassirer has said, is not merely *animal rationale*—he is emotional as well as rational—but more truly *animal symbolicum*, the user of symbols.[11] Symbols stand not for objects directly but rather for concepts of objects; unlike signs, they entail the capacity for abstract thought.[12] Expressed in language, concepts become words.[13] Only man uses symbols because only man thinks abstractly; an animal cannot distinguish the sign of an object from the object itself.[14]

Thus, largely through language, man's whole world is permeated with symbols created by culture. Indeed, some thinkers question whether we experience reality directly at all. Cassirer, for instance, writes in a celebrated passage:

[11] Ernst Cassirer, *An Essay on Man*, Yale University Press, 1944, p. 26. As opposed to a sign, whose meaning is inherent in its physical form or context and is apprehended in a sound, an odor, or a shape, the meaning of a symbol is bestowed on it by man and is comprehended intellectually. A word, for instance, is a symbol, whereas a tone of voice is a sign. If I cry, "Help!" the note of terror in my voice is a sign of distress, but the sound of the word itself—its particular combination of vowels and consonants—stands for a concept that the culture has assigned to it.

[12] Suzanne Langer, *Philosophy in a New Key*, Harvard University Press, 1951, p. 61: "To conceive a thing or situation, is not the same thing as to 'react toward it' overtly, or to be aware of its presence. In talking *about* things we have conceptions of them, not the things themselves; and *it is the conceptions, not the things, that symbols directly 'mean.' "*

[13] Symbols are expressed not only in words but also, for example, in rituals, artifacts, works of art, and gestures. Fireworks on the Fourth of July symbolize the winning of independence; the Star of David represents the identity of a people; Picasso's "Guernica" stands for the atrocities of mechanized war; the sign of the Cross portrays Christ's redemption of mankind.

[14] Take a dog whose master's name is Jim. When I say "Jim" to the dog, it receives the sound for a sign and looks for Jim, since for animals the sound of the word and the presence of the man are inseparable. But when I mention Jim to a friend, he replies, "What about Jim?", the sound bringing to his *mind* the *idea* of Jim. "That simple question," says Langer, "is forever beyond the dog; signification [i.e., sign–ification] is the only meaning a name can have—a meaning which the master's name shares with the master's smell, with his footfall, and his characteristic ring of the doorbell." Signs, then, declare their objects; symbols cause them to be conceived. Langer, *op. cit.*, p. 67.

No longer in a merely physical universe, man lives in a symbolic universe. Language, myth, art, and religion are parts of this universe. . . . No longer can man confront reality immediately; he cannot see it, as it were, face to face. . . . He has so enveloped himself in linguistic forms, in artistic images, in mythical symbols or religious rites that he cannot see or know anything except by the interposition of this artificial medium.[15]

To my mind, however, this view is overstated. Undoubtedly, a great deal of our experience is culturally patterned; yet, the keener and less controlled the sensation, as in sexual experience, the smaller is its cultural content. There is a difference, moreover, between the claim that every experience has its cultural component and the more radical, and to my mind inadmissible, assertion that every experience is culturally formed.

At this point a word is in order on language, which, being the least felt of culture's conditioners, is perhaps the most potent. Any language performs a number of functions: Through it we communicate ideas and information; we also express ourselves, release our emotions, and persuade others to act, think, and feel in ways that we prefer. More than this, language is a means of interpreting experience, leading us to look at reality in certain ways—to emphasize some of its features and ignore or discriminate among others. The structure of a language reflects certain assumptions about the nature of the world, so that our conceptions are not solely dictated by outside events but reflect, in part, what this structure has led us to observe.[16] Thus, the subject-predicate form conditions us to see a world of substances with fixed qualities rather than one of process and change. Schooled by Aristotelian

---

[15] Cassirer, op. cit., p. 25.
[16] Clyde Kluckhohn, Mirror for Man: The Relation of Anthropology to Modern Life, Whittlesey House, New York, 1949, pp. 162–163. In this respect, Clyde Kluckhohn has compared the Navaho and English languages. Navaho is generally more specific than English, although not in every respect, depending on the relative importance that speakers of the two languages attach to different features of experience. Whereas the English word "go" covers a multitude of acts and contingencies, the Navaho always specifies exactly how a man went, whether on foot or horse, by train, car, boat, plane, and so on. If by boat, the Navaho states whether he is propelling the boat himself or whether it is borne by the current or powered in some other way. If by horse, he indicates the animal's speed by the verb that he uses. He also distinguishes betwen starting to go, going, arriving and returning. On the other

logic, we maintain that something either is or is not. We refer to such clearly distinguished entities as *mind* and *body*, *good* and *bad*, whereas in the world itself things mental and physical, good and bad seem inextricably fused.

The transmission of culture depends not only on man's highly developed ability to use symbols but also on his plasticity and, hence, on his capacity for education. Unlike the animal, which for the most part responds to its environment instinctively, man has to learn how to use and adapt to his surroundings. The very inadequacy of his instincts has forced him to evolve through trial and error his own solutions to the problems of living and to hand them on to his descendants, who, lacking instinctive solutions of their own, perforce must learn this heritage too. As Durkheim has stated:

To say that innate characteristics are for the most part very general is to say that they are very malleable, very flexible, since they can assume very different forms. Between the vague potentialities which constitute man at the moment of birth and the well-defined character he must become in order to play a useful role in society, the distance is, then, considerable. It is this distance that education has to make the child travel. One sees that a vast field is open to its influence.[17]

Indeed, it is man's seeming unpreparedness for life that makes progress possible. So much of an animal's behavior is determined by instinct that it cannot improve its way of life; man, on the other hand, who must learn how to live, can also learn how to live better.

Culture for and Against Man

Culture both frees man and restrains him. It restricts his freedom of action both externally (through law and sanctions) and internally (through habit and conscience) in order to create the social order necessary for human life at all. It limits man also by permitting him to develop only a fraction of his full potential. Indeed, A. L. Kroeber comes to the astounding conclusion that no culture

---

hand, he is much less precise than the English speaker in his distinction of time. Indeed, Western man's long preoccupation with time is reflected in the complicated tense systems of European languages.

[17] Emile Durkheim, *Education and Society*, Free Press of Glencoe, New York, 1956, pp. 84–85.

fosters more than 2 or 3 per cent of man's creative potential.[18] Some cultures develop man's propensity for worship; others, his bent for art; still others, his capacity for war. Our own culture encourages, among other things, man's desire to amass wealth and display it in material objects.[19]

On the other hand, culture liberates man by providing ready solutions for many of his problems, thus releasing his energies for more creative purposes. Because of culture we know what to expect of other people and what they expect of us. Because of culture we know that we and other people attach the same meanings to the same things. Because of culture we are spared, on innumerable occasions, from deciding what to do. From culture we inherit various ways of dealing with life, such as language, religion, science, medicine, and morality, which we would hardly have invented from our own experience. Culture, in short, gives us what Gordon Allport has called "a prearranged design for living." [20]

Culture liberates, too, by creating outlets for men's energies, which enable them to be consummated satisfactorily. For instance, it enriches human experience by offering recreation and esthetic enjoyment as alternatives to the mere gratification of organic desires. To a degree, also, through medicine and technology, culture frees man from the despotism of nature and from the drudgery of toil. Printing, penicillin, the radio, the airplane, the anaesthetic— indeed, the whole range of medical and technological inventions —have made possible a measure of freedom and a release from pain and labor that the unaided individual could never have attained.

Often the same element of culture liberates and restrains simultaneously. Consider language. On the one hand, language is restrictive; it compels us to make certain sounds rather than others and to observe the rules of grammar, syntax, and spelling. On the

---

[18] A. L. Kroeber, *Configurations of Culture Growth*, University of California Press, Berkeley, 1944.
[19] Jules Henry, *Culture Against Man*, Random House, New York, 1963, Chapter 2. Henry observes that in doing so, American culture dulls man's sensitivity and imagination by training him to find satisfaction not in self-devised activities, but rather in the unceasing consumption of manufactured goods and services, the products of an economy that year by year must produce more and more if it is not to break down completely.
[20] Gordon W. Allport, *Pattern and Growth in Personality*, Holt, Rinehart and Winston, New York, 1961, p. 167.

other, it is language that permits us to express ourselves at all. It is language, indeed, that distinguishes us from the animals and delivers us from the bondage of instinct.[21]

If man cannot fulfill himself without culture, and if culture cannot exist without restraints on the acts of individuals, then cultural restraint is justified insofar as it leads to self-fulfillment. But particular cultures can restrain too much. They can seek discipline as an end in itself or perpetuate an inequitable class system. Thus, the restraints are no longer proportionate to the self-fulfillment they make possible. The more a culture is dominated by a single idea, the more it restricts the behavior of its members. The Indians of the Pacific Northwest devote much of their energy to winning prestige through lavish displays of wealth and through securing advantageous matches for their children, whereas the Plains Indians strive for prestige through deeds of war. Each of these cultures restrains its members by channeling their energies toward a single overwhelming end.

CULTURE AND PERSONALITY

Unless its members think, feel, and act alike in many different situations, a culture cannot maintain itself. What produces this conformity? In part, it is the use of rewards and punishments that encourage certain forms of conduct and deter others. Mainly, however, it is the process of enculturation by which various kinds of culturally required behavior are made to satisfy personal needs— the process, in other words, by which the impersonal goals of culture are transformed into the private goals of individuals. This second factor, the interadjustment of the individual personality and the cultural whole, forms the subject matter of the branch of anthropology known as culture-and-personality.[22]

---

21 Cf. Dorothy Lee, *Freedom and Culture*, Prentice-Hall, Englewood Cliffs, New Jersey, 1959, pp 2–3.

22 The germ of culture–and–personality is Durkheim's insight that culture actually is internalized within the personality itself. Yet, the formal study of culture–and–personality did not begin until the 1930's under the inspiration of an essay of Edward Sapir ["The Emergence of the Concept of Personality in a Study of Cultures," *Journal of Social Psychology*, V (1934), 408–415]. At first, in this field psychoanalysis overshadowed anthropology, and many pioneers of culture–and–personality, such as Erich Fromm, Abram Kardiner, and Erik Erikson, were themselves psychoanalysts.

Culture-and-personality is the meeting ground of psychology and anthropology. It reminds us that we cannot properly understand individual behavior without taking into account its cultural setting and components, nor comprehend the institutions of culture without a knowledge of the individuals who participate in them. It counteracts the psychologist's inclination to concentrate on the individual either alone or in relation to a few select persons. It points out that since each person already embodies in miniature much of his culture, many aspects of his behavior must be explained in terms not only of the individual himself but also of the culture both outside and within him. Moreover, by demonstrating that we can observe culture only in the behavior of individuals, it offsets the tendency of other fields of anthropology to focus on patterns abstracted from individual behavior as though they existed in their own right.[23]

The initial impetus to the study of culture-and-personality came from psychoanalysis, which directed the anthropologist's attention to three important factors: the deep imprint left by the experiences of early childhood on the structure of the adult personality; the status of parents and other teachers as agents of culture; and the fact that the process of enculturation, already familiar to anthropology, is also the chief molder of the individual's personality.

Nevertheless, the ascendancy of psychoanalysis has not gone uncriticized by anthropologists. It is argued, for instance, that psychoanalytic techniques and concepts, designed as they are for the study and therapy of maladjusted individuals, must be reoriented to investigate societies of sound as well as maladjusted persons. Another objection is that psychoanalysis predisposes the anthropologist to see the frustrations of culture rather than the opportunities it offers for personal fulfillment.

This alliance of anthropology and psychoanalysis gave rise to what has been and largely still is the fundamental premise of culture-and-personality: that the methods of child training in a given culture produce, or help to produce, a personality structure cor-

---

[23] M. Brewster Smith, "Anthropology and Psychology," in John Gillin, ed., *For a Science of Social Man*, Macmillan, New York, 1954, p. 35. See also Milton Singer, "A Survey of Culture and Personality Theory and Research," in Bert Kaplan, ed., *Studying Personality Cross–Culturally*, Row, Peterson, Evanston, Illinois, 1961, p. 65; and George Devereux, "Two Types of Modal Personality Models," *ibid.*, p. 236.

responding to the culture's major values and institutions. Although those who rear the child may not realize it, the methods that they use in nursing, dressing, feeding, or putting him to sleep are all conditioning him to behave according to the values of his group and culture.[24] Thus, according to some anthropologists, the stoicism of the American Indan was a product, in part, of the rigid cradle board to which he was tied as a baby and of the confinement that he experienced in childhood. By contrast, the Pueblo societies in New Mexico and Arizona, which needed a cooperative populace to run their systems of irrigated agriculture, employed a comfortable cradle board in order to cultivate a more accommodating disposition.[25]

Some anthropologists, however, have interpreted this basic premise more broadly and, I think, more realistically. William H. Sewell, for example, has suggested that the basic factor responsible for personality development is not necessarily the particular methods or devices used in training the child, such as cradle boards or tissue paper, but rather "the whole personal-social situation in which these practices find their expression, including the attitudes and behavior of the mother.[26]

But, although childhood experience may lay the foundation of the adult personality, it by no means shapes it entirely.[27] If, as psychoanalysts maintain, a child grows up secure and well-adjusted because his parents have reared him affectionately and within limits permissively, he has nevertheless received only the *basis* for a well-adjusted adulthood; whether or not he remains adjusted depends on experiences to come. The Navaho child, for instance, is highly indulged for the first two years of his life; yet,

24 Clyde Kluckhohn, *Mirror for Man: The Relation of Anthropology to Modern Life*, Whittlesey House, New York, 1949, p. 202.

25 I should point out, however, that research into the relationships between specific cultural practices and specific aspects of the personality is still highly tentative. This research is complicated by the need to distinguish between the effects on the personality of (1) the culture's practices, (2) the constitutional factors of a particular child or group, and (3) the habits of a particular mother.

26 William H. Sewell, "Infant Training and the Personality of the Child," *The American Journal of Sociology*, LVIII (September 1952), 150–159.

27 Kluckhohn, *op. cit.*, p. 201:
  At any rate the total personality can only be understood in terms of total childhood experience *plus* the situational pressures of adult life.

because of the present vicissitudes of his tribe, as an adult he is characteristically very anxious.

Some Traditional Approaches to the Study of Culture-and-Personality

The main emphasis in culture-and-personality has been, and still is, on the side of culture—on the extent to which culture molds the personalities of its members to meet its own needs.[28] According to this view, it is the early years that form the pattern of the mature personality; hence, similar childhoods will produce similar adult personalities. Since culture determines what parents shall teach their children and in what ways, we may expect a given culture to produce a distinct personality type. For instance, a rapidly changing culture needs and creates a mobile and dynamic personality, even though it may also produce a number of persons who are too disorganized or who break down under the stress of change. In America this mobile personality owes much to a kind of permissive training in both the home and the school, which allows him to develop largely at his own pace.[29] Adults, in turn, tend to perpetuate this personality type by rearing their children as a rule after the manner of their own upbringing.

Thus, culture so shapes the individual that he contributes in countless ways and, for the most part, unconsciously to its own maintenance and expansion. As it enculturates each individual, it transmutes its own needs into the inner drives of its members. Modern industry, for example, could never have emerged if so-

---

28 This approach is best summarized in Ralph Linton's four postulates of the "concept of basic personality types": (1) The individual's early experiences exert a lasting effect upon his personality; (2) similar experiences will tend to produce similar personality configurations in the individuals who are subjected to them; (3) the techniques that the members of any society employ in the care and rearing of children are culturally patterned and will tend to be similar, although never identical, for various families within the society; (4) the culturally patterned techniques for the care and rearing of children differ from one society to another. See Ralph Linton's Introduction to Abram Kardiner, The Psychological Frontiers of Society, Columbia University Press, New York, 1945, p. vii.
29 Cf. Margaret Mead, "The Implications of Culture Change for Personality Development," American Journal of Orthopsychiatry, XVII, 1947, pp. 633–646.

ciety had had to force men to be punctual, orderly, and hard-working. Enculturation was necessary to convert the objective requirements of industry into promptings within the men them-selves—that is, to create, above all through the family and school, a "social character" that strove in these directions.[30]

The Configurational Approach. This approach seeks to correlate a culture's basic personality types with its major configurations.[31] Its leading exponents are Ruth Benedict and Margaret Mead. Benedict maintains that a culture's underlying configuration can be correlated with a distinct type of personality, which, therefore, influences the adoption, growth, and modification of many dif-ferent elements within the culture. As a rule, she defines these configurations by applying to whole populations terms that psy-chologists apply to individuals.[32] In *Patterns of Culture* she classi-fies the Dobu as "paranoid" and the Kwakiutl as "megalomaniac paranoid," although she also calls the Zuñi "Apollonian" and the Plains Indians "Dionysian."

Whereas Benedict postulates a single personality type per cul-ture, Mead discovers several.[33] Into each culture, she declares, there are born a range of temperamental types, genetic and consti-tutional, of which only a few are permitted to develop, and those in accord with the culture's basic configurations. As a result, tem-peraments, fairly plastic at birth, are molded to the culture's dominant personality types, so that most adults "fit" the types that the culture requires.[34]

---

30 Cf. Erich Fromm *The Sane Society,* Routledge and Kegal Paul, London, 1956, pp. 79–80.
31 Cf. John M. W. Whiting and Irvin L. Child, *Child Training and Person-ality: A Cross–Cultural Study,* Yale University Press, New Haven, 1953, p. 2.
32 Ruth Benedict, "Configurations of Culture in North America," *American Anthropologist,* XXXIV (1932), 24: "Cultures . . . are individual psychology thrown large upon the screen, given gigantic proportions and a long time span." Such configurations, however, come dangerously close to being stereo-types.
33 Margaret Mead, *Male and Female: A Study of the Sexes in a Changing World,* Morrow, New York, 1949.
34 The configurational approach has been criticized on the grounds that, in emphasizing one or a few approved personality types, it underestimates the varieties of individual behavior that a culture tolerates. See Melville J. Herskovits, *Cultural Anthropology,* Knopf, New York, 1955, p. 3. One should note, however, that Mead and Benedict were speaking of simple cultures.

The Modal Approach. Some writers, like Abram Kardiner, regard basic personality not as a psychological type fitted to the culture's dominant values but rather as one that is founded on certain unconscious dispositions (toward parents especially) formed by the culture's primary institutions, such as its methods of child training and its family organization.[35] These dispositions persist throughout life, being projected into other people and situations and into the culture's secondary institutions, such as art, religion, law, government, and mythology.

Earlier, however, Ralph Linton had maintained that the resulting basic personality may be modified by the statuses and roles that a person assumes as an adult.[36] Indeed, these statuses and roles may produce distinct sub-types or variants of the culture's characteristic personality. Thus, each individual has a "basic personality," consisting of cultural universals learned in his childhood and a number of "status personalities" appropriate to whatever roles he plays.[37]

The Socialization Approach. David Riesman's typology of character reflects the influence of the approaches thus far mentioned, since it assumes that adult personality is fixed by the socialization patterns of childhood and adolescence, which, in turn, reflect the

[35] Abram Kardiner, *The Individual and His Society: The Psychodynamics of Primitive Social Organization,* Columbia University Press, New York, 1939; and *The Psychological Frontiers of Society,* Columbia University Press, New York, 1945. See also Melville J. Herskovits, *Cultural Anthropology,* Knopf, New York, 1955, p. 337.

[36] As Linton points out in *The Study of Man* (1936), each person occupies a certain "status" or social position, such as that of teacher, lawyer, or father, his "role" being whatever behavior society expects of someone holding this status. Increasing with a man's age, statuses are defined from infancy by his sex, perhaps by his sibling order, by his class, and by other statuses and roles that he acquires. Some statuses are "ascribed," that is, fixed and unchangeable; others "achieved," that is, chosen and attained through effort.

[37] Ralph Linton, *The Cultural Background of Personality,* Appleton-Century, New York, 1945, p. 130: Within a culture ". . . characteristic personality subtypes may develop from the differing situations of the lives of persons who play different roles in a given group." Linton calls these "status personalities" and defines them as "status-linked response configurations."

demand of culture.[38] In *The Lonely Crowd* he examines the social and psychological consequences of the transition from an early industrial to an affluent society—consequences to be seen most clearly in the pattern of life of the urbanized American middle class. In an affluent society he says, parents are more permissive and exercise less direct control over their children. Thus, the child tends to internalize no strong values from his parents but rather to take his standards from his peers. He grows into an adult with no firmly rooted moral principles and adheres more or less completely to the mores of the groups to which he belongs.

Riesman distinguishes three types of characters produced by three kinds of societies. "Tradition-directed man," at his "purest" in the primitive tribe, is hardly aware of himself as an individual distinct from his society; what he is and what he wants are determined almost wholly by the community. "Inner-directed man," such as the nineteenth century *bourgeois*, internalizes the cultural norms implanted in him at home and school, so that he comes to think of them as his own and strives hard to realize them. "Other-directed man," found increasingly in the American middle class and to some extent in the middle classes of other industrial nations, absorbs his values from his contemporaries. All goals that men pursue spring from their cultures, but, whereas the inner-directed man has internalized these goals, those sought by the other-directed man are external to him, and he is consequently more dependent on the groups in whom they are represented. Since the inner-directed man is convinced of the validity of his goals, he can ignore the demands of his peers; not so the other-directed man,

---

[38] Although he is not strictly an anthropologist, Riesman is nevertheless of great interest to anthropologists, partly because his descriptions of "inner-" and "other-directedness" as a theme in the American national character are an important contribution to our understanding of American cultural behavior, partly because his method of interviewing carefully selected informants in order to build up his hypotheses is similar to the way in which anthropologists reconstruct cultural wholes at a distance from fragmentary materials and a few living informants. See Margaret Mead, "National Character and the Science of Anthropology," in Seymour Martin Lipset and Leo Lowenthal, eds., *Culture and Social Character: The Work of David Riesman Reviewed*, Free Press of Glencoe, New York, 1961, pp. 15–26.

who, lacking compelling goals of his own, adjusts his standards to those of the groups with whom he lives and works.

In emphasizing the dominance of culture over the individual, Riesman follows the traditional approach to culture-and-personality. Like tradition-direction, both inner-direction and other-direction are patterns of conformity, one to the internalized parents, the other to the external peer group. Although Riesman is generally optimistic in his view of contemporary America, he is closer to the Freud of *Civilization and Its Discontents* than to such neo-Freudians as Erich Fromm and Karen Horney when he defines the socialized individual in terms of what society forbids him to do rather than of what it stimulates him to do.[39] In contrast to Fromm, who believes that culture as such is necessary to the fulfillment of man's deepest needs (even though particular cultures may thwart them), Riesman's typology implies that culture is hostile to individuality and to men's basic drives.[40]

Criticism of Traditional Approaches

In assuming that the existence of cultural patterns is sufficient evidence of an analogous character structure in those who participate in them, traditional approaches overlook the possibility that men may conform to these patterns without necessarily possessing

---

[39] Cf. Margaret Mead's review of *The Lonely Crowd* in the *American Journal of Sociology*, LVI (March 1951), 496–497; and Robert Gutman and Dennis Wrong, "David Riesman's Typology of Character," in Seymour Martin Lipset and Leo Lowenthal, eds., *Culture and Social Character: The Work of David Riesman Reviewed*, Free Press of Glencoe, New York, 1961, p. 298.

[40] It has been pointed out that Riesman's categories are sociohistorical rather than psychological—that they apply to a social and historical context rather than to the core of the personality—and must, therefore, be translated psychologically if they are to apply to individuals. He is less interested in individual personality traits than in the patterns of behavior and ideas expressed in them, such as folkways, collective rituals, and popular ideologies. He implies, too, that a society's character type is applicable to many different temperaments and personalities. See Elaine Graham Sofer, "Inner-Direction, Other-Direction, and Autonomy: A Study of College Students," in Seymour Martin Lipset and Leo Lowenthal, eds., *Culture and Social Character: The Work of David Riesman Reviewed*, Free Press of Glencoe, New York, 1961, pp. 319, 329; and Robert Gutman and Dennis Wrong, "David Riesman's Typology of Character," *ibid.*, pp. 310–311.

characters that are "fitted" to them.[41] Moreover, a society does not necessarily get the type of personality it "needs." [42] None of the basic personalities assembled by anthropologists from data about the dominant patterns of various cultures have been shown, in fact, to form a majority among the populations concerned.[43] Indeed, it has been argued that in no society has the basic personality of any statistically representative proportion of the population yet been established. Moreover, it is difficult to see how in a complex modern society, with so many variables to measure, this personality ever could be established.[44]

Traditional approaches also underestimate the extent to which culture (or at any rate certain cultures) enable the individual to develop his unique potentialities. Emphasizing the negative, constricting aspects of culture, these approaches pay too little attention to the opportunities it offers for creative self-fulfillment.[45] Moreover, in stressing the similarity in methods of child training throughout a society, they underestimate the variety introduced into character formation by the fact that each parent transmits the culture in a slightly different way. They also underplay the fact that each person interprets the culture that he receives in the

---

[41] Robert Gutman and Dennis Wrong make this criticism of Riesman and Fromm in "David Riesman's Typology of Character," *ibid.*, pp. 306–307.

[42] *Ibid.*, p. 303.

[43] Milton Singer, "A Survey of Culture and Personality Theory and Research," in Bert Kaplan, ed., *Studying Personality Cross-Culturally*, Row, Peterson, Evanston, Illinois, 1961, pp. 40–41:

Generally speaking, the program for validating "basic personality structure," "configurational personality," and other deviations of typical personality from cultural data and social institutions has disappointed early expectations. The introduction of psychological data about individual personalities has not led to demonstrations that "a vast majority" or "the bulk" of individuals in a culture conform to a dominant personality. Some central tendencies have been revealed in the psychological data, but the "modal types" are usually far fewer than a majority of individuals and the individual variability in types is as striking as are the similarities.

[44] See Alfred R. L. Lindesmith and Anselm L. Strauss, "A Critique of Culture and Personality Writings," *American Sociological Review*, XV, No. 5 (October 1950), 587–599.

[45] Cf. Gordon W. Allport, *Becoming: Basic Considerations for a Psychology of Personality*, Yale University Press, New Haven, 1955, p. 34.

light of his own temperament and personal history.[46] As they are transmitted, these variations pave the way for further variations, because each person, in turn, helps to socialize others, whether as parent, teacher, mentor, or employer.[47]

Traditional approaches also underestimate the extent to which the social context—that is, the demands of different roles and situations—influences a person's behavior. Teachers, for example, tend to take on the traits of their profession. Indeed, they are even influenced by the grade that they teach. Thus, the mild manner of the typical primary-school teacher becomes after a while part of

---

[46] As Allport has said:

... the moral senses and life-styles of most people reach far beyond the confines of domestic and community mores in which they were first fashioned. If we look into ourselves we observe that our tribal morality seems to us somehow peripheral to our personal integrity. True, we obey conventions of modesty, decorum and self-control, and have many habits that fashion us in part as mirror-images of our home, class and cultured ways of living. But we know that we have selected, reshaped and transcended these ways to a marked degree.

And again:

That the cultural approach yields valuable facts we cannot possibly deny, for culture is indeed a major condition in becoming. Yet personal integration is always the more basic fact. While we accept certain values as propriate, as important for our own personal course of becoming, it is equally true that we are all rebels, deviants and individualists. Some elements in our culture we reject altogether; many we adopt as mere opportunistic habits, and even those elements we genuinely appropriate we refashion to fit our own personal style of life. Culture is a condition of becoming but not itself the full stencil.

Ibid., pp. 34–35, 82.

[47] Clyde Kluckhohn and Henry A. Murray, "Personality Formation: The Determinants," in Clyde Kluckhohn, Henry A. Murray, and David M. Schneider, eds., *Personality in Nature, Society and Culture*, Knopf, New York, 1959, p. 59:

Culture determines only what an individual learns as a member of a group—not so much what he learns as a private individual and as a member of a particular family. Because of these special experiences and particular constitutions, each person's selection from and reactions to cultural teachings have an individual quality. . . . But variation is also perpetuated because those who have learned later become teachers. Even the most conventional teachers will give culture a certain personal flavor in accord with their constitution and peculiar life-experiences.

her personality. Teachers in middle grades, who must handle children too mature socially to be cowed with ease and too young emotionally to be appealed to, develop a personality always alert for trouble. Teachers in the upper grades, whose authority is less challenged, are mellower and more relaxed.[48]

Newer Approaches

No distinct school of thought has yet emerged that challenges effectively the traditional approach. Nevertheless, in recent years new voices have been heard stressing both the diversity of personality types within a culture and the individual's capacity to interpret the cultural norms that he absorbs. Let us consider the approaches of George Devereux and Anthony F. Wallace, both anthropologists, and of Gordon Allport, psychologist.

In contrast to the traditional view that culturally acceptable behavior is a result of the internalization of cultural norms in childhood and adolescence, Devereux maintains that a given activity, such as churchgoing, need not necessarily satisfy a single or a culturally implanted motive; it may, in fact, gratify a wide range of genuinely subjective motives.[49] He refers, for instance, to the manifold motives that led individual Hungarians to take part in

---

[48] That there are many exceptions to these examples I readily admit, but the theoretical basis is sound enough.

[49] George Devereux, "Two Types of Modal Personality Models," in Bert Kaplan, ed., *Studying Personality Cross-Culturally*, Row, Peterson, Evanston, Illinois, 1961, pp. 236–238:

... both organized and spontaneous social movements and processes are possible not because all individuals participating in them are identically (and sociologistically) motivated, but because a variety of authentically subjective motives may seek and find an ego syntonic outlet in the same type of collective activity. This is equally true of spontaneous revolutionary movements and of extreme conformity. (italics deleted)

And again:

... a variety of differently and highly subjectively motivated individuals may find that one and the same process in society at large can provide certain long-desired gratifications. . . . Thus, people go to church for many reasons. . . . All derive some gratification from this act, even though they are not motivated by a homogeneous set of motives, nor by one massive social motive.

the rising against the Russians in 1956. Similarly, one or a few motives may power a variety of culturally permitted activities. If cultural conformity may issue from personal motives and not necessarily from internalized norms, then, by implication, role behavior, too, may be stimulated not only by the requirements of the role itself, but also by a range of motives.[50] A teacher, for instance, may coach swimming after school hours not only because he knows that a measure of extracurricular activity is expected of him, but also because he enjoys relaxing with his pupils, or because he does not want to go home, or because it reminds him of his youth, or for many other reasons.

According to Anthony F. Wallace, the basic condition of cultural conformity is not unity of interest or motive but rather the fact that each person knows what is required under various circumstances and, therefore, tends to behave accordingly. This, in turn, comes about because members of a society, by virtue of their participation in a common culture and a common education, learn similar things and share a similar picture of their culture, however differently they may interpret particular aspects of it. In Wallace's words, they share equivalent "mazeways," a mazeway being "the organized totality of learned meanings maintained by an individual organism at a given time ... the cognitive map of the individual's private world regularly evoked by perceived or remembered stimuli." A culture functions well if the mazeways of its members contain "either identical or merely equivalent meanings for standard stimuli." [51] Wallace's theory is important because it implies a more generous view of human freedom than that of traditional approaches. It regards the individual as less subject to culturally-conditioned motives and, hence, more capable of rational decision.

---

[50] Commenting on Devereux's article, Bert Kaplan writes: "A small number of different motivations may support a wide variety of different behaviors, or quite diverse motivations in different persons may be the basis for the same role behavior. Since either can be the case, motivations are emancipated from the role requirements and we are forced to seek a new conception of the relationship between the two." See Bert Kaplan, "A Final Word," in Bert Kaplan, ed., *op. cit.*, p. 663.

[51] Anthony F. Wallace, "The Psychic Unity of Human Groups," in Bert Kaplan, ed., *Studying Personality Cross-Culturally*, Row, Peterson, Evanston, 1961, pp. 131–132.

Against the orthodox emphasis on the formative influence of childhood experience, Gordon Allport suggests that there are, in fact, three stages in a person's adoption of the norms or "model" of his culture: (1) adoption of the cultural model; (2) reaction against it; and (3) "an incorporation of the revised model as a firsthand fitting of the mature personality." [52] For instance, between the ages of five and ten the child tends to be rigidly moralistic, insisting that every game be played according to the rules and every story told as it has been before. As an adolescent, on the other hand, he reacts, often vehemently, against the mores of parents, teachers, and other adults. Finally, as an adult, he blends traditional elements of his culture with purely personal preferences, producing a distinct personality similar in many ways to the personalities of other members of his society, but more individualized and self-made than advocates of the traditional approaches are ready to admit.

Culture, Personality, and Education

In order to understand and perhaps to influence cultural change, it is necessary to know how far personality types affect the development of culture, as, for example, in accepting or rejecting innovations. A person who is heavily conditioned as a child may resist changes in directions that are not culturally prescribed yet may welcome change in areas that the culture considers appropriate. We must also understand the effect, in turn, of cultural changes on these personality types, including any changes that educators themselves may introduce. To understand this, it is necessary to know how far later learnings, such as formal education, can modify the personality and how far the personality is shaped before conscious learning takes place.

Most educators believe that the school, next to the home, is the chief means of influencing the course of culture through the modification of personality types. Nevertheless, if educators are even to consider using the school in this way to achieve any concrete and *calculated* effect on the parent culture, they must

---

[52] Gordon W. Allport, *Pattern and Growth in Personality*, Holt, Rinehart and Winston, New York, 1961, p. 170.

have a much clearer and more definitive idea of the interplay of culture and personality than anthropologists have yet presented. Moreover, if and when the main American personality types are finally located (an extraordinarily difficult, perhaps impossible, undertaking), it still remains for educators and others to decide whether or not it is desirable to change them. At present, educators are far from agreed about the types of personality that are both desirable and feasible. Progressives, for instance, believe in developing a mobile personality adjusted to a rapidly changing culture, whereas conservative educators maintain that the very rapidity and pervasiveness of change make a stable personality more necessary than ever before.

However, culture-and-personality is moving away from its earlier extreme emphasis on the formative influence of childhood training toward a view that gives more weight to later institutions and conditions of life. This shift in perspective supports the argument that education cannot change a culture's characteristic type or types of personality unless other aspects of culture are changing, too. Kluckhohn, for instance, accuses progressivism of trying to remake the American personality without altering the larger culture, so that students either abandon the progressive view of things as soon as they leave school or else wage a futile struggle against the culture as a whole.[53] Competitiveness, for instance, may seem wrong on occasions; yet, educators cannot hope to produce a noncompetitive personality that will survive, because competition is so deeply rooted in the American way of life.

The traditional approach to the study of culture-and-personality accords with the emphasis of most progressive educators in one respect—namely, the conviction that elementary rather than sec-

---

[53] Clyde Kluckhohn, *Mirror for Man: The Relation of Anthropology to Modern Life*, Whittlesey House, New York, 1949, pp. 199–200:

No arbitrary change, divorced from the general emphasis of the culture, in methods of child rearing will suddenly alter adult personalities in a desired direction. This was the false assumption that underlay certain aspects of the progressive education movement. In these schools children were being prepared for a world that existed only in the dreams of certain educators. When the youngsters left the schools they either reverted naturally enough to the view of life they had absorbed in pre-school days in their families or they dissipated their energies in impotent rebellion against the pattern of the larger society.

ondary education is the most vital period for the growth of the personality. In most other respects, it is alien to progressivism, especially in its assumption that culture will tend to mold the individual to meet its needs so that the child will have little opportunity to grow according to his personal interests. The traditional approach agrees with the scientific naturalist and behaviorist view that the child is conditioned by his environment and, therefore, has little chance for self-direction. In its relativistic view that each culture develops a distinct personality to meet its own needs, the traditional approach is at odds with educational perennialism but not necessarily with essentialism.[54]

The newer approach is congenial to both progressive and existentialist educators because it emphasizes the sheer variety of personalities to which a culture may give rise.[55] Insofar as it under-

---

[54] Essentialism is a school of educational thought, having no single philosophic affiliation, which maintains that the essence of education is the mastery of prescribed subject matter. Founded in the early 1930's, when its major spokesmen included William C. Bagley, Frederick Breed, and Isaac L. Kandel, it swept to prominence again in the conservative revival in education in the 1950's. For a brief but authentic survey, see William W. Brickman, "The Essentialist Spirit in Education," *School and Society*, LXXXVI (October 11, 1958). The spirit of essentialism, says Brickman, lies more within the aims and ideals of the individual teacher or administrator than in an elaborate organization or movement. Restating its message for today, Brickman asserts:

Essentialism is a "state of mind" which recognizes the role of definite subject matter at the core of the educational program, as well as the need for knowing the capacities and interests of the learners. It places the teacher at the center of the educational universe. This teacher must have a liberal education, a scholarly knowledge of a field of learning, a deep understanding of the psychology of children and of the learning process, an ability to impart facts and ideals to the younger generation, an appreciation of the historical-philosophical foundations of education, and a serious devotion to his work. Such teachers are properly prepared to instruct the essentials of basic subject matter, the humanistic-social-scientific-esthetic heritage, to the youth of the nation. The other skills, which are on the periphery of the school, should be taught by the agencies and individuals best equipped to do so.

[55] Existentialism is a modern Continental mode of thought, originating in the work of the nineteenth century thinkers, Søren Kierkegaard and Friedrich Nietzsche. Its leading exponents are Martin Heidegger, Karl Jaspers, Gabriel Marcel and Jean-Paul Sartre. One of its main principles is that a person is wholly responsible for all his choices. I have discussed its meaning for education in my *Existentialism and Education*, Philosophical Library, New York, 1958, and Science Editions, Wiley, New York, 1964.

66 EDUCATIONAL ANTHROPOLOGY: AN INTRODUCTION

plays conditioning and stresses personal choice, it also implicitly stresses the role of reason in personal growth (this is particularly true of Wallace) and so recommends itself to perennialism.

This chapter has examined a few of the many, still very mysterious ways in which culture influences the minds and actions of its members. This examination has led to the branch of anthropology known as culture-and-personality and to some of the controversial theories it has produced. As the text proceeds, I shall have more to say on the relations between culture, personality, and education. Meantime, let me prepare the reader for an increasingly educational approach to our subject by comparing the educational systems of modern and primitive societies.

4

Education in Modern and Primitive Societies

Culture, so much vaster than the individual that no one can know more than a fraction of it, is yet so fragile that it can be almost totally transformed in a few generations. If for some reason, such as conquest by a foreign power, the young fail to receive their cultural heritage, the culture of their parents is doomed.[1] True, a culture can be revived, but the same means is used to revive as to preserve it—education. What, then, are the common characteristics of education in all cultures?

SOME UNIVERSAL CHARACTERISTICS OF EDUCATION

Almost any conscious human learning involves the three processes of listening, watching, and doing. Particular cultures vary in the emphasis they lay on one or the other of these processes and in the extent to which they stress one or the other in learning specific things. In contemporary Western education children read more than they watch or listen, although the balance is shifting slightly through the use of television as an instructional medium and because much education consists of "learning by doing." Again, American schools rely heavily on learning through questions

---

[1] The Aztec and Inca cultures, for example, lost their elites as a result of foreign invasions, and these elites have never been restored.

and answers—a method that encourages the child to think for himself, provided it is not used solely for drill—whereas the Chinese are expected to learn mostly by watching. The children of the Pilagá, on the other hand, learn a great deal by having their mistakes corrected by adults. If a child points to an object, for instance, and misnames it, any adult will put him right.[2]

All cultures use rewards and punishments to encourage learning and to correct errant behavior. The rewards vary from praise and appreciation to the presentation of prizes; the punishments, from reproof and ridicule to confinement and physical pain. As the child matures, he gradually ceases to be rewarded for conformity and is punished instead for nonconformity. What we have yet to learn is how much the child is disappointed at being rewarded no longer or how much he would feel insulted if he continued to be rewarded for something he had mastered already.[3]

All societies withhold certain crucial knowledge from children. The Chagga, for instance, maintain male superiority by informing girls that men do not defecate, whereas the Hopi tell children that the Kachina dancers are not men but gods. Modern societies tend to keep the child ignorant of sex, although he often picks up haphazard notions, usually from older children, and may experiment with this knowledge himself.

Throughout the world the adolescent peer group tends to reinforce cultural conformity. In primitive communities as well as in modern industrial societies it encourages its members to observe the moral standards of their elders, although in the latter societies it also stimulates them to rebel against their parents. It can do so in the last case because in these cultures children no longer receive their economic place in society from their parents but, as a rule, must win it for themselves.

Almost invariably the dominant group in a culture organizes the educational system to strengthen its own position. In this country, for instance, white members of the middle class run the schools at some disadvantage to Negro, Mexican, and working-class students. In England, the "public" schools, with their wide resources of

---

2 Jules Henry, "A Cross-Cultural Outline of Education," *Current Anthropology*, I, No. 4 (July 1960), 304.
3 *Ibid.*, p. 277.

patronage, are run by, and largely for the benefit of, the upper classes. In Russia the Communist party, in Ireland the Roman Catholic church dominate education.

The social standing of the teacher varies with the respect his society has for knowledge. Societies such as Japan and China, which revere knowledge, esteem their teachers more highly than European and American societies, which have less respect for knowledge as such, however much they may prize its material applications. In his book, *The Schoolmaster*, the sixteenth century English scholar, Roger Ascham, complained that the aristocracy paid their grooms more highly than the tutors of their sons. Today, professional athletes and screen actors receive more money than college professors.

MODERN AND PRIMITIVE SOCIETIES CONTRASTED

Before contrasting the educational systems of modern and primitive societies, let us first contrast the societies themselves. The classic conception of a primitive society is Robert Redfield's view of the "folk society" as an ideal type approximated by various nonurban societies (including Eskimos and Mexican peasants).[4] Such a society is small, isolated, non- or semiliterate, homogeneous, highly integrated, and consensual, with strong group solidarity and simple division of labor. Much of its behavior is familial, traditional, and relatively static. Its members tend to be "inward looking."[5]

For the philosophers of the Enlightenment, primitive societies were the setting for man in a state of nature before the creation of civil government. For nineteenth-century anthropologists, they provided the prototypes of contemporary institutions. What do they hold for anthropologists today? In the first place, the more

---

[4] Robert Redfield, "The Folk Society," *American Journal of Sociology*, LII, No. 4 (1947), 293–308.
[5] Cf. Wendell Oswalt, *Napaskiak: An Alaskan Eskimo Community*, University of Arizona Press, Tucson, 1963, p. 148:

> The folk society is a small society, nonliterate and relatively isolated, with feelings of social unity and very little division of labor beyond that based upon age and sex. It is also an integrated whole in which there is very little individualism and in which community relationships are on a highly personal basis. The urban type [of society] is represented by characteristics opposite those of the folk.

—and the more varied—the societies we study, the more likely we are to find elements common to all societies, which may enable us to plot, and perhaps control, the future course of social and cultural development. Next, being simpler and more integrated than modern societies, primitive societies are easier to grasp in their entirety; hence their study forms a suitable prologue to the consideration of more complex cultures. Finally, since they are far removed from our own culture, we can study them with more detachment than we can cultures closer to hand.

A primitive society is remarkably homogeneous; the great majority of its members share similar knowledge and interests and are familiar with the thoughts, attitudes, and activities of the entire community. In modern industrial societies—complex, specialized, and highly populated—so much information has accumulated that many people are ignorant of the very existence of certain bodies of knowledge—neurophysiology, for instance, or cybernetics. In Jules Henry's words, "As knowledge increases in any culture, ignorance tends to increase in individuals, for these come to know less and less of the total available information." This dilemma is particularly noticeable in school teachers who are expected to teach a range of subjects.[6]

The very complexity of modern cultures tends to make them less immediately sensitive than primitive communities to the impact of mass emotions. To many Westerners the primitive tribe seems almost childlike in its sudden shifts of feeling. One reason for this comparative inconstancy is that its members are less accustomed than Westerners to reflective thinking. Another is that the very homogeneity of background and outlook in primitive tribesmen encourages similar reactions to similar stimuli. In a diversified culture, however, and in a culture as pluralist as ours, the average child is exposed to a range of competing influences, such as parents, teachers, peers, and television. As a result (to exaggerate a little), no one pattern of habits roots itself deeply enough to inhibit seriously the formation in the young of fresh habits. The adult, too, is a member of many groups, such as the family, the firm, the church, and the political party, each with its own aims and modes

---

[6] Henry, *op. cit.*, p. 296. I am especially grateful to Professor Henry for much of the information in the ensuing pages.

of conduct. Thanks, moreover, to mass media, the adult is also made aware of the interests of other groups, such as labor unions, parent-teacher associations, Seventh Day Adventists, and the NAACP. When we recall, finally, that in his daily life the modern adult constantly meets members of other groups, we should have no doubt why he is more eclectic and more skeptical in his beliefs than the primitive tribesman who is dominated by the mores of a single community. On the other hand, as two world wars have shown, so-called civilized societies are by no means immune to mass emotions, even hysteria.

In modern societies the typical family unit is the simple or nuclear family, consisting of the married couple and their children. In most primitive societies, however, the unit is the extended family or kin group, comprising several generations held together through the male line, as in traditional China, or the female line, as in the Navaho. The kin group generally shares a common dwelling place, each smaller family living in a hut or apartment of its own.

Among modern beliefs one of the most fundamental, and one of the most far-reaching in its effects, is the belief in progress. For modern man the future is, with few limitations, open. He believes that through the application of science to nature and human relations the condition of mankind, both physical and spiritual, can be improved almost immeasurably. For primitive man, on the other hand, the scheme of things is immutable. Man and his environment form an indivisible whole. Nature is to be served, not exploited. The American Indians, for example, believed that in hunting certain animals both the hunter and his prey cooperated with nature in a sacred activity, man furnishing the ceremonial, the animal offering his flesh.[7]

In primitive tribes the individual exists only as a member of his community, which is adapted to the unchanging order of things. By following the ways of the community the individual survives and prospers. Indeed, some tribes, like the Wintu Indians, have no notion of the self as a separate entity.[8] Modern man is socially more isolated. With the growth of urbanism, which encourages mobility

---

[7] Dorothy Lee, *Freedom and Culture*, Prentice-Hall, Englewood Cliffs, New Jersey, 1959, p. 163.
[8] *Ibid.*, pp. 132–140.

and specialization and weakens the ties of kin, the average man is in actual touch with a mere fraction of all the groups in his society, and he has a partial understanding of only a few of his culture's activities. This fact gives rise to one of the great responsibilities of any modern educational system—namely, to introduce the young, however briefly, to that vast terrain of culture that they normally will never encounter at first hand.

Whereas nearly all the members of a primitive community share the same basic assumptions, in an advanced society people can differ on profound issues without destroying the unity of the whole culture. The Civil War, for instance, may have sundered American society but it did not cleave American culture.

Whereas a primitive society satisfies certain known and relatively fixed needs, a modern industrial society must constantly create new needs in order to keep its economy in motion. Since this economy generally restyles old products and manufactures new ones faster than the consumer demands them, it must create an elaborate system of advertising in order to keep demand abreast of production. The primitive workman, on the other hand, produces what things are needed when they are needed. Since the demand for his wares is relatively settled, he needs neither advertising nor salesmanship. Thus, a primitive society is stable because its members' needs are relatively finite, but a modern society is necessarily restless and dynamic, since it assumes that the needs of its members are infinite.[9]

Modern Western societies theoretically set no limit to the property that a man may accumulate (although they may tax him heavily once he has accumulated it!); hence our unceasing quest for wealth. In contrast, most primitive societies restrict the amount of property that a single person may amass privately, and people use a variety of means to rid themselves of their culturally unacceptable surplus, such as exchanging it ritually, distributing it to relatives, burning it at funerals, and using it to pay for ceremonies.[10]

Work enters more deeply into the life of primitive man than it does into that of the modern worker. Not only does it bind the

---

[9] Cf. Jules Henry, *Culture Against Man*, Random House, New York, 1963, pp. 8–9, 17–18.
[10] Cf. *Ibid.*, pp. 9–10.

members of the tribe together in the performance of tasks whose social significance is clear to all, but it also enables them to express themselves creatively. Molding a pot or embellishing a harpoon, primitive man can indulge a loving care and an instinct for decoration that have little place on the modern assembly line. The modern industrial worker generally does a routine job requiring little intellect, imagination, or initiative, and one that fosters few qualities of value to the society outside his place of work. He develops little sense of loyalty to his fellow workers, largely because whatever they work to produce is not shared amongst them but rather disposed of by the organization that employs them. In the modern world, it is largely the professional man and the executive who are emotionally committed to their jobs; the worker, as a rule, is involved mostly in the private world of his family and friends and, less frequently, with his labor union.

Since a primitive society judges everything by established principles, it tends to change very gradually. Hence, some modifications of tradition—in a dance step, say, or a style of ornament—which a Westerner may barely perceive, may well seem revolutionary to primitive man. Sudden and drastic change—the result perhaps of natural disaster or Western intervention—may overwhelm his culture completely. I say "may" advisedly, because some primitive cultures, such as the Manus of New Guinea, have been remarkably adept at adapting to Western ways.[11] Advanced and complex cultures, on the other hand, must, of their very nature, tolerate differences and ambiguities and, hence, rapid change.

MODERN AND PRIMITIVE EDUCATION CONTRASTED

Unlike the modern child, the primitive youngster shares actively in communal life. From an early age he is expected to take responsibilities commensurate with his strength and experience, particularly by helping his family to acquire its livelihood. Boys, for instance, hunt and trap smaller game, and girls assist in the fields or look after younger siblings. Since the primitive society has less specialized knowledge and fewer skills to transmit, and

---

[11] Margaret Mead, *New Lives for Old: Cultural Transformation—Manus, 1928–1953*, Morrow, New York, 1956. See also Wendell Oswalt, *Napaskiak: An Alaskan Eskimo Community*, University of Arizona Press, Tucson, 1963.

since its way of life is enacted before the eyes of all, it has no need to create a separate institution of education such as the school.[12] Instead, the child acquires the heritage of his culture by observing and imitating adults in such activities as rituals, hunts, festivals, cultivation, and harvesting. As a result, there is little or none of that alienation of young from old so marked in modern industrial societies.

A further reason for this alienation [13] is that in his conception of reality the modern adult owes less to his direct experience and more to the experience of his culture than does primitive man. Clearly, his debt to culture will vary with the nature and extent of his education. Nevertheless, the man in the street today takes for granted many facts about the world which he himself could never have discovered. Hence, in order to acquire the technology and world view of his elders, the contemporary child must travel much further than the offspring of primitive man. He is, therefore, that much more removed from the adults of his society.

In primitive cultures the formal agents of education include the family, the kin, and ceremonial initiations. The school comes comparatively late in the history of a culture, and in some cultures not at all. Various conditions have summoned the school into existence: (1) the development of institutional religion and the need to train a priesthood; (2) internal growth or conquest abroad, requiring the preparation of civil and military administrators; (3) the division of labor, calling for instruction in special techniques and, in industrial societies, necessitating a basic literacy as the prerequisite of vocational skills; (4) conflicts within society, which threaten traditional values and beliefs and lead to the use of education to reinforce acceptance of the heritage.[14] An anthropological study of American educational practice might very well base itself on these four factors, substituting politics and civic leaders (or civil servants) for religion and the priesthood.

---

[12] In most primitive societies, however, adolescents are formally trained and tested in the *rites de passage,* ceremonies that initiate them into adult life.
[13] I shall examine others in later chapters.
[14] One sample of such a conflict in America today is the controversy over whether patriotism should be indoctrinated, allowed to develop with the natural course of events, or analyzed critically.

However, the transmission of culture is never entrusted to the school alone. In America today, social workers, psychiatrists, nurses, recreationists, and others are all deliberately created agents of formal education. Next, there is a range of institutions that educate deliberately but nevertheless informally, in that none has been formed for the purpose of education alone. These include the family—still the main agency of education in its fullest sense —the church, the peer group, and the media of mass communication. For their educative influence on the adult we may add such institutions as the workshop, the social class, the voluntary organization, and the armed services. Finally, although it is not itself an institution, there is the climate of opinion in society as a whole, which can often be tyrannical.

Modern education also separates children from their parents. In primitive societies, whether the teacher is a parent, a maternal uncle, a family elder, or a shaman, education seeks to maintain an unbroken continuity between the generations. Today's schools, on the other hand, are dedicated to raising the child's expectations beyond those of his parents, turning the sons of laborers and clerks into doctors, lawyers, and financiers.[15]

One of the most striking differences between education in primitive and in advanced societies is the shift from the need of an individual to learn something that everyone agrees he wishes to know to what Margaret Mead calls "the will of some individual to teach something which it is not agreed that anyone has any desire to know." [16] The primitive child goes to a relative or perhaps to an expert in his tribe to learn all that he can about some particular activity, such as hunting, fishing, or trapping, and its significance in the lore of his tribe. He learns not only because it is universally agreed that there are certain things he should know but also because he himself, seeing their immediate relation to his present and future life, wishes to know them. He learns, in short, in order to survive—learns, for instance, which paths to follow and which

---

15 Cf. Margaret Mead, "Our Educational Emphases in Primitive Perspective," in George D. Spindler, ed., *Education and Culture: Anthropological Approaches*, Holt, Rinehart and Winston, New York, 1963, p. 316.
16 *Ibid.*, p. 311.

to avoid, which berries are edible and which are poisonous. Accompanying his father, the son learns to hunt by actually killing animals, and his sister learns how to bring up a family by sharing the household duties with her mother.

The modern child's apathy toward education has precisely the opposite cause—his inability to connect the information that he acquires in school with what he must know in order to work productively and enjoy himself in the course of his life. Whereas the primitive child is always in close touch with the adult version of the skill that he is learning, the modern pupil generally is physically and psychologically removed from the offices and factories that will use the knowledge and skills he is taught. Failing to see any immediate practicality in school learning, he often becomes listless and unruly. Indeed, this indifference to education is the mainspring of the pervasive indiscipline of American schools; if children could see more immediate value in what they were learning, they would be more eager to learn it.

Yet much hinges on the concept of interest. The primitive child's interest in what so clearly and closely relates to him is no longer possible for the modern student. The task of education now is to awaken intellectual curiosity—an interest in knowledge as such apart from its practical application. This is not easy, for it demands from the child a detachment, a discipline, and a play of intellect that do not come to him immediately but that are, nevertheless, the hallmarks of civilized man. Let us by all means acknowledge the seemingly more spontaneous discipline of primitive children, but let us not imagine that the moral and intellectual development required of modern man can be attained painlessly.

A primitive community contains no one whose sole function is to teach. The older members instruct their younger kin, although for specific purposes, such as training for the priesthood, individual adults may be nominated. As a result, those who teach participate fully in the communal life. Among more advanced cultures the sheer weight of knowledge to be taught brings into being the professional teacher, who, in the contemporary West, tends increasingly to be cut off from the main industrial and commercial life of his society. Like other citizens he reaps the benefits and the ills of specialization—greater knowledge and expertise on the one hand, narrower spheres of operation on the other. It is strange, is it not, that in most Western cultures teachers are blamed for being "too theoretical," too "out of touch with reality," when at the same time they are discouraged from outside activities on the grounds that such activities interfere with their profession. Even their direct participation in politics is frowned upon. Americans are especially suspicious of teachers who "moonlight," even though they realize that most of them do so in order to earn enough additional money to support their families.

Primitive teachers practice what they teach; hunters teach archery and spear throwing, farmers agriculture, and so on. In modern societies, most of what the teacher practices is teaching. A high-school teacher of economics, for instance, cannot also be an executive in a corporation or an advertising agency. Having no more to teach than what he daily practices, the primitive teacher easily marries teaching with doing.

Moreover, the primitive teacher is deeply committed not only to his pupil, who is probably a member of his own kin, but also to the results of his teaching. If he fails to communicate his skills effectively, he feels the consequences almost at once. If a boy is not taught properly how to hunt, his teacher may go hungry. The Western teacher, not implicated directly in his students' subsequent success or failure, lacks this life-or-death incentive to teach efficiently.[17]

In a primitive society teaching and learning come more easily because the object of instruction is constantly available, whether it be a spear, a plow, or a ceremonial mask. (Nevertheless, in a number of primitive communities there is also a vast reservoir of esoteric knowledge that must be transmitted intelligibly, since this lore is believed to insure the community's survival and fecundity.) The American teacher, on the other hand, must explain things that are far removed in space and time both from himself and from his pupil, such as *Hamlet*, nuclear fission, and the slave trade. If he imparts such knowledge as ancient history, he must try to explain its relevance to modern life.

[17] Cf. Jules Henry, "A Cross-Cultural Outline of Education," *Current Anthropology*, I, No. 4 (July 1960), 296–297.

In a very primitive society, like that of the Eskimo, education does not last long. By the time he is nine years old the Eskimo child has learned from his parents how to speak the language, how to handle tools, and how to predict the weather. He has also been familiarized with certain personal relationships and religious taboos. As he matures, he will become more proficient in hunting and in his knowledge of weather and the environment. But his formal education has finished in the sense that he has now learned whatever adults can teach him directly.[18]

The greater the knowledge and the more complex the skills required for cultural life, the longer education takes. A modern society teaches its children more knowledge than a primitive one, uses more varied teaching methods, and spends more time on formal instruction, though probably less time on each subject taught. With more to learn than his primitive counterpart the modern child is under greater pressure from teachers and parents to master the subjects prescribed for his age in the time allotted them. The official writ may be that each American child is to learn a new subject only when he is ready for it; in fact, however, he is constantly being urged toward culturally determined standards of attainment rather than standards set by his own temperament and talents. The familiar phenomenon of mental blackout may well be the result of overloading the child's abilities. In Henry's words, we "jam the machine" and bring on "blackboard paralysis."[19]

One reason that we study the educational methods of primitive cultures is to acquire a more balanced and critical view of our own educational system. Clearly, we cannot transplant primitive practices into our own vastly more complex culture and expect them to work, for we would be removing them from the only context in which they make sense. On the other hand, the success that primitive peoples have had in managing certain aspects of

---

[18] Margaret Mead, "Why Is Education Obsolescent?" in Ronald Gross, ed., *The Teacher and the Taught: Education in Theory and Practice from Plato to James B. Conant,* Dell, New York, 1963, p. 268.

[19] This happens, says Henry, "when there is a critical moment in the educational process at which massive pressures are brought to bear on a child to perform an incompletely mastered task within a narrowly limited time." Henry, *op. cit.,* p. 278.

their educational life should encourage us to tackle our own problems with greater perspective and optimism. I refer in particular to such problems as integrating the child into the adult community and arousing his interest in being educated. These two points, among others, form the substance of the next chapter.[20]

---

[20] At many points in this chapter I have deliberately simplified my generalizations in order to present the material as clearly and succinctly as possible. The reader should bear in mind that a closer study of primitive communities would lead to more qualifications than are mentioned here.

5

Education and Cultural Change

CULTURAL CHANGE AND CULTURAL LAG

Culture is constant yet always changing—constant in that certain of its elements, such as language and law, persist without major alteration for long periods of time; changing in that all its elements, however gradually and subtly, are undergoing a continuous metamorphosis. Cultural change includes three main processes known to anthropologists as *origination, diffusion,* and *reinterpretation.* Origination is the discovery or invention of new elements within the culture. Progressive education, for instance, originated for the most part in the United States. Diffusion is the borrowing of new elements from other cultures, such as the adoption of the Italian Montessori method by American educators. Reinterpretation is the modification of an existing element to meet fresh circumstances, as in the extension of federal aid to education.

Unless it is very highly integrated, a culture does not react as a whole to any single change, however important. The mutation of some major aspect of culture will sooner or later affect almost every other aspect, but it need not affect them all equally or immediately. For example, the discovery of nuclear power transformed almost overnight the popular attitude to war, but it has yet to influence the nation's use of fuel or its concept of political sovereignty.

The concept of *cultural lag* signifies the tendency of some areas of culture to change more slowly than others. Consider the most obvious form of cultural lag in this country, the discrepancy between technology and values.[1]

Although some anthropologists traditionally have assumed a sharp division between a society's technology and its values, technology is, in fact, pervaded by values, since new technological devices and processes are linked through their functions to the forms of conduct that a society approves. The automobile exemplifies the values of social mobility, private property, and the love of speed. The thermometer and the clock testify to the conviction that nature can and should be measured, that all such units of measurement are of equal worth, that life is governed by knowable and invariable laws, and that what can be observed and repeated is important.[2]

We may thus envision two orders of cultural values, which may or may not coincide. One is fed by innovations in technology; the other is the sum of established values. (The latter is not always expressed in contemporary innovations but is doubtless the product in part of technological innovations in the past.) If the values expressed in technological change are compatible with established values, then the culture will adjust to the changes easily enough, no matter how rapid they are. Hence, it is not so much the rate of technological change that causes cultural disorganization as it is the extent to which this change embodies new and conflicting values.

The more integrated the culture, the more its technology and

---

[1] Technology often seems to be the most dramatic pacemaker of modern culture, largely because it changes by accumulation rather than by replacement. As a rule one technical device or process leads to another, and the rewards of change are fairly tangible, whereas a change in values or beliefs generally involves a complete substitution. As Honigmann has said, "A novelty in social organization or ideology rarely builds on previous areas of behavior but rather will encourage their replacement through substitution. In the case of techniques and their accompanying artifacts, secondary inventions are frequently added to a basic invention." John J. Honigmann, *The World of Man*, Harper, New York, 1959, p. 252. The pace of cultural change may also be set by other factors, however, such as ideology, as in modern Russia and China and in National Socialist Germany.

[2] Cf. Harold L. Hodgkinson, *Education in Social and Cultural Perspectives*, Prentice-Hall, Englewood Cliffs, New Jersey, 1962, pp. 110–141.

values are likely to interpenetrate; it is mainly in less integrated cultures, like the United States, that technology can unmoor itself from the order of established values. Thus, in earlier times and in primitive societies cultural values were expressed through the technology by which society maintained itself. For example, among the Maya Indians of southeast Yucatán agriculture is not only a means of securing food but also a way of worshipping the gods. Before planting, an Indian builds an altar in the field and prays there. The field is thus a kind of temple, which he is forbidden to profane by speaking boisterously. Planting forms part of a perpetual contract between gods and men, in which the gods grant men the fruits of the earth in return for piety and sacrifice.[3] The modern assembly line, by contrast, implicitly rejects many traditional values of the culture, notably the belief that the individual is an end in himself. On the floor of a modern plant each worker is an interchangeable part and a means to the end of production.

EDUCATION AND CULTURAL CHANGE

I stated earlier that education is a necessary condition of cultural continuity. It is also an important means of cooperating intelligently with cultural change. Thus, one way in which a society seeks to keep abreast of changes is by modifying in each generation the heritage taught in the schools. To this end educators reinterpret old knowledge and values to meet new situations. For example, since the splitting of the atom and the inauguration of the United Nations, we no longer teach either Newtonian physics or patriotism as absolutes. In addition, new knowledge and skills are added to the curriculum, and some old ones are abandoned. In this century, for instance, while jettisoning Latin and Greek, the high school has embraced the social sciences with enthusiasm; it has expanded its program of vocational training to meet the growing demand of industry for skilled workers; and it has tended, through

---

[3] Robert Redfield and Lloyd W. Warner, "Cultural Anthropology and Modern Agriculture," *Farmers in a Changing World, 1940 Yearbook of Agriculture,* United States Government Printing Office, Washington, D. C. Quoted by Dorothy Lee, *Freedom and Culture,* Prentice-Hall, Englewood Cliffs, New Jersey, 1959, p. 166.

greater emphasis on natural science, to encourage a more experimental temper of mind.

A culture may also seek to anticipate the future by implanting in the young certain information, attitudes, and skills designed to meet specific foreseen situations. In recent years, for instance, this country has increased its spending on scientific education in general and on the education of engineers in particular in order to surpass the Soviet Union in the exploration of space.

Education may, in addition, be an inadvertent source of cultural change. Each culture conditions its members to act, think, and perceive in what the anthropologist calls a "culturally delimited universe," consisting of the world that the culture itself has created and those aspects of the physical universe that it has chosen to find significant. "We may speculate," writes Jules Henry, "that very stable cultures have perfected, or nearly perfected, the process of narrowing the child's perceptual field—of training the child to dismiss from his mind anything not selected for his perceptions by the culture." [4] Yet, not even the most extreme totalitarianism can completely limit the child's understanding. The discrepancy between what the child is supposed to learn and what, in fact, he does learn is an important source of conflict and change within a culture. For example, many an authoritarian school is breeding rebellious spirits who will later reform the educational system that offended them.

Granted that we can use education to cooperate with cultural change, can we also use education to influence or control it? Contemporary educational theorists have answered this question in three ways. Let us examine each answer and see to what extent it has the support of anthropology.

Educational Progressivism

Progressive education, as commonly understood, offers a *via media* between the two views that educational change is wholly dependent on social change and that education can reform itself and

---

[4] Jules Henry, "A Cross-Cultural Outline of Education," *Current Anthropology*, I, No. 4 (July 1960), 275.

society without the necessary cooperation of social forces.[5] Its main thesis is that, although education cannot determine the direction of social change (since by itself it cannot exert sufficient leverage against the countervailing cultural forces), it can nevertheless develop a mentality capable of dealing with change when it occurs—that is, it can teach children to react to change intelligently. In this way society will be educated to improve itself without the need for teachers to convince the young of specific changes that they, the teachers, believe to be desirable. To this end children must study and resolve situations taken from real life that they themselves find genuinely problematic. From this experience they will acquire the necessary intellectual and emotional dispositions, as well as various specific techniques, for dealing with changes in general.[6] Such situations will be found in the study of contemporary problems mainly through the social sciences. The progressive teacher will not propose his personal solutions for the children to debate but will allow them to reach their own conclusions in accord with their own values.[7]

---

[5] Sidney Hook, *Education for Modern Man: A New Perspective*, Knopf, New York, 1963, p. 87:

> That educational changes by themselves are sufficient to effect basic social changes, and that a profound educational transformation can get under way without profound social changes, are, both of them, mistaken views. But that education can accomplish little or nothing in changing society, and that widespread reforms in education are impossible until the country lifts itself by its bootstraps, are views that are just as mistaken.

[6] *Ibid.*, p. 92:

> The decisive steps in social transformation depend upon the crises that are prepared not by education but by the development of the underlying economy, existing technology, and the chances of war. What education can do is to prepare, through proper critical methods, the attitudes and ideals that come *focally* into play when crises arise. It can develop the long-term patterns of sensibility and judgment which *may* be decisive in resolving the short-term problems whose succession constitutes so much of the substance of contemporary history.

Cf. also John L. Childs, *Education and Morals: An Experimentalist Philosophy of Education*, New York, Appleton-Century-Crofts, 1950, p. 114.

[7] Hook, *op. cit.*, p. 111: For those educators who still desire a more direct and specific influence on society Sidney Hook suggests two extra steps: helping students to find congenial employment and obtaining a place on national agencies of social and economic planning.

The progressive educator rejects any scheme for using the school to inculcate a program of social reform, maintaining that such "indoctrination" infringes on the free play of the child's intelligence and so limits his growth. He also opposes any attempt to specify exactly what the good society must be on the grounds that the future is too uncertain. Claiming that his philosophy of education is the most democratic of all, he advocates a society that plans itself as it evolves rather than one that is planned in advance.

To my knowledge, no anthropologist has yet endorsed the progressive view of the school's responsibility with regard to social change. Nevertheless, the notion that the school should deliberately foster a mentality attuned to change is *prima facie* in harmony with the views of such anthropologists as Anthony F. C. Wallace, who believe that rapid change need not be psychologically harmful but may produce a variety of personality types.[8] It is necessarily at odds with the views of those anthropologists who maintain that rapid change tends to disrupt the personality.[9]

Educational Conservatism

According to conservative educators (such as perennialists and essentialists), the school cannot force the pace of social change without perverting its true function, which is to train the intellect.

---

[8] Anthony F. C. Wallace, *Culture and Personality*, Random House, New York, 1961, p. 119:

> Now it is possible that when the culture is "heterogeneous" and rapidly changing, there will be a wider variety of personality types produced than in the homogeneous, slowly changing culture. Each of these types may be as consistent internally as any type produced in a stable homogeneous culture. The problem of such a complex society will not be that all of its members have split personalities, but rather that the problems of sociocultural organization may exceed the capacities of its members. Under the latter eventuality, many individuals may experience privation and frustration and come to suffer from psychosomatic and neurotic complaints; but these will be the consequences of failure of the system to answer the wants of certain of its members.

[9] E.g. Margaret Mead, "The Implications of Culture Change for Personality Development," *American Journal of Orthopsychiatry*, XVII (1947), 633–646; and Ernest Beaglehole, "Cultural Complexity and Psychological Problems," in Patrick Mullahy, ed., *A Study of Interpersonal Relations*, Hermitage House, New York, 1949.

The school is not properly a reforming body but an institution of learning. Since it is individuals who transform society rather than vice versa, the true way to improve society is by improving the individuals within it.[10]

In this view, the school is responsible for inculcating in the student what is permanently worthwhile in the culture's heritage and for adjusting him to society as it now stands. If the school is turned into an agency of cultural reform, it will prepare the student for a milieu that may never be realized, instead of fitting him for the conditions under which he must actually earn a living.[11] Moreover, the high-school student has neither the experience nor the sophistication to weigh questions of social and cultural reform. It is particularly pointless to expect him to judge the problems of the contemporary culture according to his own values, not only because his values are immature, but also because such problems must be considered in the light of the culture's fundamental values, which are an essential part of its heritage and, hence, an unsuitable topic for school debate.[12]

To make the school a reforming agency would also deliver it into the hands of competing interest groups. Constantly under pressure to provide a hearing for all kinds of programs and policies, constantly pestered by cranks and fanatics, the school would degenerate into something little better than a political lobby. Thus, Hutchins writes:

If one admits the possibility of obtaining through the school social re-

---

[10] Robert M. Hutchins, *The Conflict in Education in a Democratic Society*, Harper, New York, 1953, p. 69: "Society is to be improved, not by forcing a program of social reform down its throat, through the schools or otherwise, but by the improvement of the individuals who compose it." The reader should remember that the word "improve" is value-laden. *All* educators want to improve the individual; how they will do so depends on their theory of values. Similarly, all educators want the school to aim for "excellence"; what this excellence consists of will depend on their idea of the good. The repetition of such words as "improve" and "excellence" by those who, unlike Hutchins, have no theory of values and no idea of the good is pointless.

[11] Isaac L. Kandel, *Conflicting Theories of Education*, Macmillan, New York, 1939, p. 32: The prime purpose of education is to "reproduce the type, to transmit the social heritage, and to adjust the individual to society."

[12] Cf. Robert M. Hutchins, *op. cit.*, pp. 50–51.

forms that one likes, one must also admit the possibility of obtaining social reforms that one dislikes. What happens will depend on the popularity of various reformers, the plausibility of their causes, and the pressures they are able to exert on the educational system.[13]

Reconstructionism

The essence of reconstructionism is that educators themselves must rebuild society by teaching the young a program of social reform at once detailed and all-embracing. Reconstructionism claims to remedy three "failings" of progressivism: a lack of goals; an undue emphasis on individualism; and an underestimation of the cultural obstacles to social change.

Progressivism, says Theodore Brameld, fails to postulate any clear-cut ends for social action, partly because it is fascinated by the process rather than the ends of thought and partly because it believes that the universality of change invalidates any firm commitment to specific long-term goals.[14] Fundamentally, he says, progressivism would have the school cultivate the individual intelligence. Although progressives insist on the need to use this intelligence cooperatively, they specify no ends for which men should cooperate. Progressivism, declares Brameld, misconceives society to be an aggregate of individuals. It overlooks the supraindividual nature of many forces and institutions, such as socioeconomic classes, mass media, pressure groups, and other centers of power in society. It understresses the persistence and recurrence of cultural patterns and, therefore, overemphasizes the novelty of history, the opportunities for unplanned change, and the inevitability of progress.[15] It does not see that broad social changes must be planned rationally well in advance and executed with all available resources.

The new society must harmonize the basic values of Western

---

[13] *Ibid.*, pp. 52–53.
[14] Theodore Brameld, *Education for the Emerging Age: Newer Ends and Stronger Means*, Harper, New York, 1961, p. 34: "Like the American culture of which it is the ideological ally, it [progressivism] has been much more concerned to delineate an effective methodology of intelligent practice than to formulate the goals for which the methodology is indispensable."
[15] Cf. Theodore Brameld, *Philosophies of Education in Cultural Perspective*, Dryden, New York, 1955, pp. 183–189.

culture with the driving forces of the modern world. It must be a democracy whose major institutions and resources—industry, transport, health, and so forth—are publicly controlled.[16] The logical goal of national democracies is a democratic world government in which all states participate.

According to Brameld, the school must convince its pupils that the reconstructionist program is both valid and urgent, yet it must do so democratically or deny the principle of democracy that it claims to uphold. The teacher must encourage his pupils to examine the evidence for and against reconstructionism; he must present alternative proposals scrupulously; and he must allow the children to argue their own views publicly. The final decision whether to accept reconstructionism or not must be left to the pupils themselves. In Brameld's words:

We are teacher-citizens with convictions, with commitments, with partialities that we believe are defensible. And we mean not only to exhibit these in the public square, not only to invite completely free inspection of each conviction, but to work for their acceptance by the largest possible majority.[17]

Nevertheless, he believes that the reconstructionist program will win the pupil's allegiance on its own merits.

Reconstructionism has won much attention but little support. It has been criticized as too ambitious. To chart the future in such detail is to ignore two well-known facts: one, that time outmodes all but the most general schemes of long-range reform; the other, that any realized reform is the product of compromise and mutual adjustment and, hence, it bears little relation to the design of its first mover. Reconstructionism, it is also said, overlooks the realities of contemporary politics, notably that no government will allow its schools to be used to promote a point of view that it opposes. Moreover, in the very breadth and novelty of the changes that it advocates reconstructionism falls into the same error it im-

---

[16] Theodore Brameld, *Toward a Reconstructed Philosophy of Education*, Dryden, New York, 1956, pp. 328–329: "Control by the largest possible majority of the principal institutions and resources of any culture is the supreme test of democracy . . . the working people should control all principal institutions and resources if the world is to become genuinely democratic."
[17] *Ibid.*, p. 338.

putes to progressivism—it underestimates the extent to which deeply entrenched cultural patterns mold the ways in which people conceive and implement change.[18] Furthermore, in inviting the student to accept a program of social reform that society has not yet approved, reconstructionism can only alienate him from his culture, from his elders, and from those of his own generation who have not attended reconstructionist schools.[19]

A number of other criticisms may be made of any attempt, like reconstructionism, to use education to create a new social order. Since one of the main motors of cultural growth is technoeconomic change, it follows that, if we wish to redirect society, we must control, or at any rate influence, the rate and direction of technoeconomic developments. This is clearly beyond the unaided capacity of education. The alternative is to let technology blaze the trail for culture to follow and to counteract the cultural lag by allowing education to raise the rate of change of the culture's values. Again, one may doubt whether education by itself can do this. Even if it could, such rapid change in values would place too much strain on the individual's personality.[20]

In my own view, reconstructionism is at fault because, in making the school an instrument of social reform, it narrows the scope of education. A reformist school will almost certainly limit its teaching to the kinds of knowledge likely to support its case. Even if it does not, the inculcation of reform is still likely to deprive other areas of education of their due attention—which is bad enough. Moreover, education is only one institution among many; it cannot push through a program of reform against a coalition of other interests, such as labor, business, and the church. More important, formal education can only scratch the surface of social and cultural change, whose real springs lie much deeper in such

---

18 Cf. George D. Spindler's review of Theodore Brameld, *The Remaking of a Culture*, in *Harvard Educational Review*, XXXI, No. 3 (Summer 1961), 348.
19 Knowing Professor Brameld, I am sure that he would not be too disturbed by this last criticism. Nor would I. For different reasons both of us believe that a healthy alienation from much of modern society by intellectually and psychologically capable individuals would be a desirable countermove against unexamined collectivization.
20 Cf. Harold L. Hodgkinson, *Education in Social and Cultural Perspectives*, Prentice-Hall, Englewood Cliffs, New Jersey, 1962, p. 111.

events as war and invasion, revolution, class antagonism, technological innovation, and mass migration.[21]

Views of Some Anthropologists

Few anthropologists will applaud a plan to make the school a van-
guard of social reform against other powerful social and cultural
forces. Despite Brameld's pioneering work in educational anthropology, his reconstructionist program has failed to elicit any anthropological support that I know of. On the other hand, an
equally utopian scheme for education, though one which lacks
the detailed planning that was so impressive a feature of reconstructionism, has been proposed by the anthropologist Ashley
Montagu, whose views belong to the tradition of romantic progressivism running from Rousseau's *Emile* through Friedrich Froebel
to the child-centered schools of the 1920's.

According to Montagu, the prime end of the school in our time
must be nothing less than to transform humanity by teaching the
younger generation how to "love" through an education in the "art
of human relations." The school must teach all subjects with an
eye to their "significance for human relations." [22] It must encourage students to evaluate the world "humanely and critically," not
merely to echo their parents and teachers. It must cease to inculcate the values of an industrial society, such as competition and
material success, and promote instead such values as patience,
cooperation, charity, and peace of mind. More than this, since a
new order will not be built on good intentions alone, the school
must also teach its students, as part of their training in human
relations, what society now is and why and how it must be
changed.[23]

If the school is to make the child a loving person, says Montagu,

---

[21] Brameld himself concedes that reconstructionism seems less relevant to the
present cultural climate than it did to that of the 1950's, although he believes
that its hour will yet return. See his *Education for the Emerging Age: Newer
Ends and Stronger Means*, Harper, New York, 1961, p. 1.

[22] Ashley Montagu, *Education and Human Relations*, Grove Press, New York,
1958, p. 22: "An intelligence that is not humane is the most dangerous thing
in the world."

[23] *Ibid.*, pp. 28–29, 95.

it must enroll him from his earliest days. Although the home plays a leading role in the formation of personality, human relations are better taught in the school, because many parents, being emotionally frustrated, are inefficient teachers. All children, therefore, should attend public nursery schools. Since, in addition, as mothers, women are fitted by nature to be more loving than men, they should take the leading part in teaching and reforming mankind.[24]

Objections to this plan are contained in the critique of reconstructionism. Let me mention two more. First, nowhere in his book does Montagu list any specific social reforms. If society is to be put right and if the school is to show its pupils how to do so, then we need something more concrete than the proposal that certain contemporary values should be exchanged for others. Secondly, Montagu ignores the crucial question of how he is to persuade an industrial society engaged in a worldwide struggle for power and influence to adopt an educational system that is explicitly anticompetitive.

Most anthropologists, and not only those who see culture as superorganic, maintain that education cannot direct social change, because it is already interwoven with more powerful social and cultural forces. Ruth Benedict, for example, declares that education cannot mitigate rapid change, since the latter is the result of factors in the culture deeper and more pervasive than education itself:

Our problems in transmission of culture arise from the rapidity of social changes in our society; and no method of education can prevent this. . . . Those critics who blame education for the changes they resent in our culture are making the educational system a scapegoat for vast changes in the structure of modern society which they do not take into account.[25]

W. Lloyd Warner argues that education must necessarily reflect existing social conditions, or it will fail in its task of adjusting the coming generation to the social and cultural milieu in which it

---

[24] *Ibid.*, pp. 22, 95, 163–164. For Montagu preparation for motherhood would form the core of a girl's education.

[25] Ruth Benedict, "Transmitting our Democratic Heritage in the Schools," in Blaine E. Mercer and Edwin R. Carr, eds., *Education and the Social Order*, Rinehart, New York, 1957, p. 213.

must live. No matter how noble the ideals inculcated by the school, if they are at odds with this milieu, they are bound to harm the child.[26]

Anthony F. C. Wallace maintains that education serves the needs of three kinds of societies—the "revolutionary," the "conservative," and the "reactionary." [27] He says that a revolutionary society, such as China or Cuba, seeks totally to transform its culture. It needs to revitalize its population morally and to create a dedicated, intellectually resourceful elite, which will handle the task of transformation. Hence, its education will emphasize first morality (especially loyalty and self-sacrifice), then intellectual training, and lastly technical skills. In a conservative society, such as Britain or the United States, whose main concern is to maintain and improve an established order, neither intellect nor morality plays such a vital role. Here education will tend to concentrate on technical skills, on "how to do" certain things, such as driving, accounting, voting intelligently, and handling people efficiently. A reactionary society, such as Portugal or South Africa, challenged by revolutionary movements, shores up the traditional values that are under attack by making morality the focus of its education system. It thus tends to circumscribe intellectual, though not technical, training. Wallace sees certain tendencies to reaction in American culture. He mentions the educator's excessive preoccupation with technical skills, shown in courses in driving, sex, and marriage, and the increased concern with "morality" manifested in loyalty oaths, book censorship, and the investigation of teachers and scientists. He urges Americans to resist these tendencies by redirecting the school to its former task of liberal intellectual training.

---

[26] W. L. Warner, Robert J. Havighurst, and Martin B. Loeb, *Who Shall Be Educated?* Harper, New York, 1944, p. 143:

> As long as we have our present social structure, education must be adapted to it, or we will produce a generation or more of maladjusted children and unhappy adults. The school in America, whether we like it or not, must function to make democracy work in a status system that is only partially equalitarian. Only as our social order changes can the school indoctrinate its pupils with economic and political philosophies of human relationship which are now in sharp conflict with the prevailing social system.

[27] Anthony F. C. Wallace, "Schools in Revolutionary and Conservative Societies," in Frederick C. Gruber, ed., *Anthropology and Education*, University of Pennsylvania Press, 1961, pp. 25–54.

Thus, most anthropologists agree with conservative educators that the school has little or no independent influence on social and cultural change. This view is ably expressed by an English educator, A. K. C. Ottoway. Education, he argues, can produce changes in culture and society only under orders from those in power.[28] In totalitarian countries especially, education can transform the attitudes of an entire generation, but only because it is directed to do so by the ruling party. Education can also prepare the young for change by encouraging the habit of independent judgment. But, again, it can do so only when such judgment is already valued by society at large.[29]

In sum, most commentators are agreed that the school cannot by itself influence the course of social and cultural change, although it can foster a personality type that is amenable to the rapid changes endemic in industrial societies. Today, in the United States both the elementary and the high school are mainly concerned to transmit the culture's heritage. The university, on the other hand, besides transmitting the heritage, also discovers new knowledge and examines and criticizes society. The university, therefore, not only adjusts to culture but also adds to it. In addition, it influences the culture in an indirect way by attempting to make people more knowledgeable and, hence, (one hopes) more tolerant. Finally, it helps to differentiate the culture by educating

---

[28] A. K. C. Ottoway, *Education and Society: An Introduction to the Sociology of Education,* Routledge and Kegan Paul, London, 1953, p. 56:

> In general it may be said that the education a society provides, at a given time, is determined by the dominant social forces at work in that society. Social forces are defined as groups of people trying to bring about social action or social change. As the nature of society changes, through the interplay of social needs, techniques and values, so education tends to follow. The question will be asked: is not education itself a social force? In one sense, yes. It is a force which supports and develops the changes in social aims already decided by those in power, but it does not initiate the changes.

[29] *Ibid.,* p. 12:

> In a democratic society . . . education, used in a particular way, can *prepare* for changes in society, and that is part of its creative function. It prepares children for change by encouraging permissive and critical attitudes, but it can only do this because these are already sufficiently accepted values of society.

people for different occupations. There is a case, therefore, for saying that the university at least exercises a small, unspecific, but nevertheless beneficial, influence on a culture's development. This does not mean, however, that our schools should not strive much harder to make their influence felt. A learning society is a desirable thing from any point of view. If it can do nothing else, education can train leaders in all walks of life to be more intellectually aware of the multiple forces that shape the progress and welfare of culture here and elsewhere.

6

Education and Discontinuity

One of the most striking features of the process of enculturation in modern industrial societies is the sharp separation of the mature from the immature personality. In a variety of ways these societies distinguish the behavior and values appropriate to children from the attitudes and conduct that they expect of adults. In these societies every young person faces an abrupt major discontinuity in the process of growing up. During adolescence he must switch with little preparation from the ways prescribed for the child to those prescribed for the adult. For many to whom the 'teens are already a period of disturbing biological and psychological change, the added burden of moving from one way of life to another constitutes an acute and prolonged strain.

Not all societies deliberately dislocate the process of growth. In many primitive societies, such as the Samoan, the Arapesh, and the Hopi, the course of enculturation runs smooth and continuous, permitting the child to mature gradually without sudden or severe strain. Instead of confronting him suddenly with the demands of adulthood, they bring him along through various stages, each with its appropriate role. The Kalingas of the Philippines recognize as many as ten stages: "newborn," "beginning to smile," "he creeps," "he sits alone," "he stands up," "he begins to walk," "he runs around," "he can be sent on errands," "he can be sent to the forest for fuel," and finally "companion," signifying that he has come of age and can fight, court, marry, and set up a household.[1] Moreover, with some exceptions, such stages tend not to be sharply distinguished.[2]

In contrast to the United States, where most parents constantly exhort their children to compete academically and socially with other children of the same age, some primitive societies allow the child to mature at his own pace, permitting him, for example, to be initiated into adulthood when he is ready for it and not necessarily when he has reached a certain age.[3] Many primitive societies, it is true, provide a protracted and often painful initiation into adulthood; yet, the ordeal is nearly always deliberately devised and carefully controlled to reorient the adolescent from one way of life to another, whereas the ordeal of the modern adolescent confuses rather than reorients him.

DISCONTINUITIES IN AMERICAN CULTURE

The most pervasive discontinuity experienced by the American child is that between his family and the wider world. In few, if any, cultures is the family so detached from kin and community. Lacking the support of older kin and communal lore, the American family seems uniquely isolated and burdened with responsibilities. Moreover, in a society that has grown steadily more competitive and more impersonal, marriage is increasingly regarded as a haven of security and affection. Today parents have children out of love, not, as previously, for a financial investment. Whereas formerly the child was considered to have an obligation to his parents, parents now feel obliged to sacrifice for their chil

[1] Ina Corinne Brown, *Understanding Other Cultures*, Prentice-Hall, Englewood Cliffs, New Jersey, 1962, p. 50.

[2] E.g., among the Mixtecans of Juxtlahuaca in Mexico the ascent to adulthood is continuous except for fairly sharp transitions from (1) infancy to early childhood, marked by abrupt weaning and a change from sleeping with parents to sleeping alone or with siblings, and (2) early to late childhood, characterized by greater expectations of responsibility, obedience, and self-reliance. Kimball Romney and Romaine Romney, "The Mixtecans of Juxtlahuaca, Mexico," in Beatrice B. Whiting, ed., *Six Cultures: Studies of Child Rearing*, Wiley, New York, 1963, p. 630.

[3] See William F. Nydegger and Corinne Nydegger, "Tarong: An Ilacos Barrio in the Philippines," *ibid.*, p. 820.

dren.[4] Until he goes to school, the child lives almost wholly within this family. As a rule, the only other adults that he encounters are certain relatives and the mothers (rarely fathers) of the playmates he visits. Thus, early in life his expectations of older people are shaped almost entirely by his parents and older siblings.[5]

By contrast, in the extended families of most primitive societies the child mingles with people of all ages and experiences. In many such societies adults raise their children together, so that all the children belong, in effect, to all the households. If the child wants a plaything fixed or a drink of water, he may go home or to grandparents or to a wide range of "aunts" and "uncles." If he misbehaves, any adult may chastise him.[6] Neither school (if he attends one) nor adulthood introduces him to spheres of activity that he knows nothing about, because he is acquainted already with people who move within them. Since his family participates more fully than the American family in the life of the community (in such activities as cultivation, worshipping, feasting, burying, and harvesting), he early encounters people in the different roles and statuses that his society provides.[7]

More than this, during his preschool years the American child is brought up almost entirely by one person, his mother. It is mainly she who disciplines him, rewards him, and loves him. Gone most of the day, his father is both less real to him and less influential. Schoolchildren have only the vaguest ideas of their father's occupation, even though they recognize that he provides the family with subsistence, security, and social position.[8] Inevitably, the

---

[4] Cf. Grace Graham, *The Public School in the American Community,* Harper and Row, New York, 1963, pp. 159–160.

[5] Cf. John L. Fischer and Ann Fischer, "The New Englanders of Orchard Town, U.S.A.," in Whiting, *op. cit.,* p. 967.

[6] Cf. Nydegger and Nydegger, *op. cit.,* pp. 834–835.

[7] George D. Spindler, "Personality, Sociocultural System, and Education among the Menomini," in George D. Spindler, ed., *Education and Culture: Anthropological Approaches,* Holt, Rinehart and Winston, New York, 1963, p. 381. According to Spindler, by the age of five a child of the Menomini Indians is "at least dimly aware" of all the roles and statuses in his tribe.

[8] Nevertheless, whenever they *are* at home, many fathers still exercise authority over their preschool children, either taking sole charge of discipline or (less frequently) sharing it with their wives. Cf. Fischer and Fischer, *op. cit.,* pp. 971–972.

child has difficulty in adjusting himself to other people, because for his first five years he has depended so heavily on his mother. Moreover, even when the father plays a substantial role in the household, the child is still relatively limited in his social contacts by this prolonged enclosure in the tiny world of his family.[9]

In many primitive societies, on the other hand, the child is reared by a variety of relatives, and in all primitive societies he is cared for much of the time by older siblings.[10]

In contemporary America childhood and adulthood are also sharply separated because the child assumes no social or economic responsibility.[11] In towns especially, his play does not prepare him for an occupation. Moreover, the shift from an agrarian to an industrial society has made social competence at once more necessary and yet, for the child, more difficult to obtain, for the growing length and increasing abstraction of his education, together with the ever more complex technical nature of work itself, remove him yet further from the processes by which men earn their living. Except among the lowest income groups, the money that he earns as a paper boy or golf caddy is either of marginal importance to his family or else enters his own pocket. In fact, his parents may well pay him to do chores that in previous ages he would have performed as a matter of duty. Hence, he contributes nothing significant to society by working. Indeed, he is forbidden to work full time; yet, as soon as he reaches maturity, he is expected to compete on equal terms with other adults.

In many primitive societies work and play involve the same activities. At birth a Cheyenne Indian is given a small bow and arrows and, as he grows older, receives bigger ones. When he brings home his first snow bird, his family hold a feast in celebration, even if on the same day his father brings home a buffalo. In such societies children quickly develop a sense of responsibility by sharing the family tasks at an early age. Among the Navaho, children from about five on are given sheep of their own to look after, so that they can supply meat for family meals and, on occasions,

9 Cf. Spindler, op. cit., pp. 381–382.
10 Cf. Nydegger and Nydegger, op. cit., pp. 820–821.
11 Ruth Benedict, "Continuities and Discontinuities in Cultural Conditioning," in W. Martin and C. Stendler, eds., Readings in Child Development, Harcourt, Brace, New York, 1954, pp. 142–148.

for ceremonies.[12] In Samoa, girls often no older than six look after younger siblings and, when not acting as nursemaids, work on plantations and help carry food to the village. Young boys, too, learn the simpler elements of canoeing and reef fishing. As the children grow older and stronger, they assume tasks requiring greater skill. Unlike the American child, they grow into responsibility by taking it in degrees from the beginning.[13]

In contrast to the primitive child who, at the age of six or less, may be looking after a younger sibling, an American child is generally twelve years old at least before he is allowed to take full charge of a younger child.[14] Most parents feel that a child of less than twelve will be irresponsible and will find the task too onerous. They also fear the criticism of neighbors, who frown upon the idea of very young baby-sitters.

In America, also, children are expected to be submissive, adults dominant. As a result, the adolescent is caught between the habit of submitting to adults and the need to be self-assertive in order to behave like an adult himself.[15] The conflict is particularly acute for a young married couple who must make a family of their own only shortly after leaving their parental homes. The girl, accustomed to being looked after by the boy as well as by her parents, must suddenly take responsibility for the health and welfare of a husband and children. The boy, in the habit of indulging himself, must now consider the needs of an entire household.

In some primitive societies, on the other hand, the child is permitted more self-assertion and, therefore, grows more easily toward adult dominance.[16] In Samoa, the influence of parents is limited. Discipline is the task of older siblings, and the six- or seven-year-old girl, who as nursemaid dominates her younger

---

[12] Dorothy Lee, *Freedom and Culture*, Prentice-Hall, Englewood Cliffs, New Jersey, 1959, p. 11.
[13] Margaret Mead, *Coming of Age in Samoa*, New American Library, New York, 1950.
[14] Cf. Fischer and Fischer, *op. cit.*, pp. 946, 965.
[15] Ruth Benedict, *op. cit.*, pp. 142–148.
[16] *Ibid.*, p. 145. Benedict mentions a Crow Indian who boasted of "his son's intractability even when it was the father himself who was flouted; 'He will be a man,' his father said. He would have been baffled at the idea that his child should show behavior which would obviously make him a poor creature in the eyes of his fellows if he used it [this kind of behavior] as an adult."

siblings, may herself be dominated by older sisters. The older she grows, the more children she disciplines and the fewer who discipline her. Hence, step by step she acquires the dominant personality expected of an adult. In Samoa, too, if a youth quarrels with his parents, instead of remaining under the same roof to feud with them, as he would in our society, he moves without opprobrium to his uncle's house or village. The Navaho treat both adults and children as equal. The Navaho child is not ordered to keep his hands off sharp knives or to stay out of reach of the fire but is allowed to learn from his own mistakes. He is not forced to go to school or hospital; he makes up his mind for himself. The following indicident illustrates the Navaho's respect for the child's autonomy. Questioned by an anthropologist, a Navaho woman once told him that a certain baby could talk. Seeing the anthropologist's bewilderment at the meaningless sounds the baby was uttering, she confessed that she could not understand what the baby was saying, but she would not take it on herself to admit that the baby was not really talking.[17]

Finally, there is a discontinuity in our culture between the freedom of the adult to release his impulses and the self-control expected of the child. Adults may smoke, drink, tell racy stories, and engage in sexual intercourse. Children may not. Our culture is particularly severe in its repression of youthful sexuality. It teaches the child that sex is wrong, and, having in his teens informed him of the facts of reproduction, it forbids him to experiment with what he has learned. Pregnancy is camouflaged, breast-feeding is hidden, and many girls menstruate for the first time in ignorance of its meaning. Virginity and continence are extolled, but on the wedding night the woman is supposed to be sexually intelligent and responsive, and the man skilled enough to reassure her.

Not all cultures separate the child from the adult so sharply. Among the Pilagá Indians of Argentina children may enjoy sexual intercourse, listen to and tell sexual stories, and smoke when tobacco is available They drink little, not because drinking is held to be immoral but because it is reserved for older men.[18] In Samoa, sex is considered natural and pleasurable. The young Samoan may

---

[17] Dorothy Lee, op. cit., pp. 12–13.
[18] Cf. Jules Henry, Culture Against Man, Random House, New York, 1963, p. 237.

experiment freely with different sexual practices, only incest being prohibited. Indeed, the Samoan girl often postpones marriage in order to prolong the sexual freedom of adolescence. Sexual deviations, which lead in this country to neuroses because of the moral and social stigma they carry, in Samoa carry no appreciable stigma whatever.

I am not arguing that we should allow our children to smoke, drink, and be promiscuous. Far from it. Our culture requires a much more sophisticated level of behavior than is needed among the Pilagá or the Samoans, and, consequently, the techniques of competent adult behavior are less easily and less quickly acquired. With good reason we teach our children to restrain impulses that we permit adults to express, for children lack experience to count the consequences of emotional release. On the other hand, there is nothing sacrosanct about the precise limits that we currently place on the behavior of our children. The child is constantly aware that his parents are freely expressing impulses that he is supposed to restrain, and this awareness not only taxes his self-control but also leads to deceit and feelings of guilt. How much of this strain is necessary and, indeed, salutary and how much can be avoided is matter for debate. What cannot be doubted is that our increasingly hedonistic culture is granting its children an ever growing measure of emotional freedom, and both parents and teachers would do well to learn to cope more effectively with the inevitable consequences.[19]

The Modern Adolescent

Yet, suppose these discontinuities did not exist. Living as he does in a complex and swiftly changing culture, the modern youth would still be subject to greater strain than youth in primitive societies, since he has more, and also more complicated, choices to make and, hence, runs more risk of choosing inappropriately. The

---

[19] Ibid.:
The discontinuity between child and adult behavior in this regard [i.e., controlling the impulses] is disappearing, however, not only because it is difficult to maintain but because the world, including the parents, offers no rewards for self-restraint and no satisfying substitutes for "indulgence."

anxieties of decision are multiplied, too, not only by the existence of conflicting moral and social standards but also by our belief in the importance of choice and in the individual's responsibility for the consequences of his behavior.[20] Another source of stress is the fact that children mature physiologically earlier than they used to, with the result that they take up certain activities, such as dating and going steady, when they are psychologically less prepared for them.

This earlier imitation of adult behavior, together with the increasing duration of education, serves to prolong the period of social adolescence and to create a mass adolescent subculture characterized by conformity to the peer group and hostility or indifference to parental values. Centering on the high school, this separate culture, whose members rely on one another for psychological support and social reward, "maintains only a few threads of connection with the outside adult society." [21] Among boys popularity goes to the athlete, the car owner, and the boy from the right family; among girls to the one with poise, manners, looks, or clothes. For both sexes academic success is much less important than teachers would like to think.

In this subculture, which is largely created for him by adults (advertisers, manufacturers, and the operators of the mass media), the adolescent feels removed from the world of his parents. What-

---

[20] Cf. Margaret Mead, *Coming of Age in Samoa*, American Library, New York, 1950, p. 154. See also her essay, "The Young Adult," in E. Ginzberg, ed., *Values and Ideals of American Youth*, Columbia University Press, New York, 1961. Mead writes that the emphasis of American culture on dating adds to the anxieties of the adolescent, who often as not lacks firm values of his own and so feels unable to resist the group's pressure on him to engage in sexual activities that he may not really desire. Boys, in particular, who mature more slowly than girls, are often forced into female company for which they are ready neither physiologically nor psychologically. Instead of making deep friendships with members of their own sex, they come to distrust other males as competitors for girls. According to Mead, this premature heterosexual association leads to antagonism between the sexes, to "hostility to females on the boys' part and, on the girls' part pressure toward marriage combined with contempt for males" (p. 79).

[21] J. S. Coleman, *The Adolescent Society*, The Free Press of Glencoe, New York, 1961, p. 3. See also C. Wayne Gordon, *Social System of the High School*, Free Press of Glencoe, New York, 1957.

ever antagonism he may feel toward his parents is intensified by certain other important factors, of which I will mention a few.

First, the pace of social and cultural change outmodes the knowledge and attitudes of parents more quickly than it used to. The modern adolescent is all the more aware that his parents' standards are "dated" because the mass media daily provide him with the latest styles of teen behavior, with its own evanescent customs and special argot. Second, economic specialization has helped to alienate father from son, partly because the son need no longer follow his father's career, partly because, even if he does, the knowledge and skills that he must learn will probably be too complex for his father to have time or inclination to teach him. Third, family cohesion is weakened, because the adolescent contributes nothing substantial to the family's economy and also because the family rarely teaches him any specific knowledge or skills that fit him for a role in the adult community. Finally, in a swiftly changing and pluralist society he is exposed to the conflicting values of a range of religious and secular systems—an experience that undermines still further whatever convictions he may have acquired as a child. Feeling that the standards of his elders are irrelevant to his world, he turns for reassurance to his peers, not thereby attaining real independence but merely changing the environment to which he conforms.

EDUCATION AND CULTURALLY INDUCED DISCONTINUITIES

In such circumstances what attitude should the educator take toward culturally induced discontinuities in the pupil's emotional and intellectual development? Let us consider, in turn, the training of character and the training of intellect.

Discontinuity and Character Training

Believing, as they do, in human plasticity and the depth of cultural conditioning, most anthropologists regard the problems of adolescence as the result of cultural pressures. Psychoanalyists, on the other hand, consider them to be mainly biological in origin. Hence, anthropologists tend to be more optimistic that the difficulties of adolescence can be circumvented if only the cultural patterns inducing them can be modified. They caution the educator against accepting too readily the idea that contemporary problems, such as those of the modern adolescent, are the inevitable lot of mankind as a whole.[22]

In Margaret Mead's early writings this point of view appears in an extreme form. There she maintains that the stresses and strains of growing up result solely from the demands of the culture and have no biological basis whatever. "At whatever point the society decides to stress a particular adjustment," she writes, "it will be at this point that adjustment becomes acute to the individual." [23] She instances the variety of attitudes toward, and ways of dealing with, menstruation in a range of cultures, including that of Samoa where it is no problem at all. More recently, however, she has conceded that there are some basic regularities in human development with which every culture must come to terms.[24]

The views of Mead and Benedict on culturally induced discontinuity imply that in the home and also in the school—where, it is said, childhood dependence is prolonged artificially in order to facilitate discipline—the child should be treated more as a potential adult, assimilating values and behavior similar to those that will be expected of him in maturity and, above all, learning nothing that, as an adult, he will have to abandon. How is this to be done?

Rejecting outright any return to a more primitive way of life, Mead advocates more freedom for the young (especially the adolescent) from the expectations of family, peers, and community, so that each person may realize more fully his particular talents. If, she says, we base our educational practice on an under-

---

[22] Franz Boas, *Anthropology and Modern Life*, Norton, New York, 1928, p. 185. 'It is necessary that the crises and struggles that are characteristic of individual life in our society be investigated in societies in which our restraints do not exist while others may be present, before we assume all too readily that these are inherent in 'human nature.' "

[23] Margaret Mead, "Adolescence in Modern and in Primitive Society," in G. E. Swanson, T. M. Newcomb, E. L. Hartley et al., eds., *Readings in Social Psychology*, Holt, New York, 1952, p. 537. (Originally in V. F. Calverton and S. D. Schmalhausen, eds., *The New Generation*, Macauley, New York, 1930.)

[24] Margaret Mead, *Male and Female*, Morrow, New York, 1949, pp. 143, 176.

standing of the child's growth, both psychological and physiological, and on a knowledge of the patterns of culture, we can permit a much greater development of individual differences and, in this way, contribute to the growth of culture itself.[25] Here she implicitly endorses the view that the only way for the school to influence the general movement of culture is by educating for a flexible personality.

Since the school can only continue what the family has already begun, Mead calls for a more flexible family. With its strong and intimate ties, she says, the American family interferes too much with the young person's growth, preventing him from the full use of his own resources. In her own words, "It would be desirable to mitigate, at least in some slight measure, the strong role which parents play in children's lives and so eliminate one of the most powerful accidental factors in the choices of any individual life" [26] The best way, she says, to build a well-adjusted personality is to have a tolerant family whose members can disagree without emotional tension.[27]

Progressivism. On this question of discontinuity the views of Mead and Benedict come close to those of progressive education. In calling on the school to take responsibility for character training, which it claims the family is no longer suited to provide, progressivism advocates what is, in fact, a much freer upbringing for the child, since the modern American school, being nonauthoritarian and more detached from the child than his parents, will be less liable to mold his personality in any set direction. Progressivism is also opposed to the discontinuity between childhood submissiveness and adult dominance, for it advocates that from the beginning of their lives children should exercise a growing measure of free-

---

[25] Margaret Mead and F. C. Macgregor, *Growth and Culture*, Putnam, New York, 1951, p. 185. "We can attempt to alter our whole culture and especially our child-rearing patterns, so as to incorporate within them a greater freedom for and expectation of variations."

[26] Margaret Mead, *Coming of Age in Samoa*, New American Library, New York, 1950, p. 141.

[27] Margaret Mead, "What Is Happening to the American Family?" *Journal of Social Casework*, XXVIII (1947), 330. It is not the family as such that Mead censures but rather the particular pattern of the American family that, she alleges, produces conformity and dependence in its children.

dom and responsibility. The teacher's role, it says, is not to command but to cooperate with the pupils largely as they feel they need him.

In opposing this discontinuity, however, does the progressive educator deny his own principle that the child should be treated according to the needs and desires of his age? Not at all, he replies. The pupil should be granted more freedom of expression, movement, and behavior if only because he cannot be expected to manifest the consistency and self-direction of the adult, which are the fruit of greater experience. Now, if we deal in this way with the childlike nature of the pupil instead of imposing on him the discipline we expect of an adult, we, in fact, make his growth more continuous, for we do not require him to shift suddenly from being controlled by others to directing himself as an adult. The progressive educator maintains, too, that the child should study what interests him rather than what a teacher believes he should study—a procedure that, once again, gives the child more freedom and responsibility and so removes him less from the adult state.

The progressive educator would also make the school responsible for the social conditioning of the child by teaching him, for example, how to behave toward the opposite sex. Most probably, the progressive school would bring the child to social maturity earlier than would his parents—a condition that would ease his transition to adulthood by accustoming him for a longer time to certain forms of adult behavior.

Progressivism also seeks to mitigate the discontinuities between the nuclear family and the wider world and so between the responsibility of the adult and the nonresponsibility of the child. In the progressive view, the task of integrating the child into the adult community can no longer be performed by the family and must now become the responsibility of the school. As John L. Childs puts it, only the school can give the child that direct acquaintance with, or "primary experience" of, the conditions of modern life that is necessary for the formation of a mature personality.[28]

---

[28] John L. Childs, *Education and Morals: An Experimentalist Philosophy of Education*, Appleton-Century-Crofts, New York, 1950, p. 147:

As the modes of living and making a living in our present day industrial

Let me now mention three ways in which, according to progressivism, the school can mediate between the young person and the larger community. In the first place, the pupil should study the "real" problems of his society, such as unemployment, crime, and urban renewal, not merely as academic exercises but rather as problems vitally affecting the environment in which he lives. To this end the social sciences should become the backbone of the school curriculum.

Second, if these problems are to be studied intimately and effectively, the teacher must have time and opportunity to take his students into the community in order to examine the problems at first hand and to talk with labor leaders, policemen, city planners, and others whose job it is to handle them. He must also be able to apply to these problems a number of disciplines and a wide range of information. This, in turn, requires a curriculum sufficiently elastic for the teacher or a group of teachers to work with the children for varying lengths of time and to use whatever materials and methods the problem may dictate.[29]

Third, if young people are to participate fully in the adult community, they must learn how to do so by sharing in the total life

---

civilization tend to limit the opportunity of the young for direct participation in the life of their society, the obligation of the school to provide a program of rich and varied primary experience becomes ever more urgent. . . . Nothing is deeper in the life of the person than his characteristic ways of responding to conditions and people, and no education meets the moral test which fails to provide for this medium of primary experience in and through which immature beings achieve the modes of their personhood.

Cf. Victor B. Lawhead, "A Curriculum for Citizenship Education," in Association for Supervision and Curriculum Development, *New Insights and the Curriculum*, National Education Association, Washington, D.C., 1963, p. 267; and I. James Quillen, "The Curriculum and the Attacks on the Public Schools," in George Z. F. Bereday and Luigi Volpicelli, eds., *Public Education in America: A New Interpretation of Purpose and Practice*, Harper, New York, 1958, pp. 120 and 124.

29 Victor B. Lawhead, *op. cit.*, p. 267:

The rigidity of the orderly fifty-minute schedule and the neatly packaged bodies of subject matter apportioned to the school day offer little opportunity for the interested teacher to involve his students with civic problems which require multidisciplinary approaches and sufficient time to utilize community resources for learning.

of the school. At present, instead of allowing children a genuine voice in school government, educators generally give them the illusion of participation through spectator sports and the like. Meantime, the students themselves, seeking more direct participation in the larger world than the curriculum affords them, must turn instead to the school's extracurricular activities, which offer many students their only contact with the life of the adult community.[30]

Conservatism. Although most American anthropologists would favor reducing the culturally induced discontinuities in a young person's experience, there are some who believe that sharp discontinuities serve a very important purpose. They agree with Durkheim that the child needs strict discipline by others if he is to learn to discipline himself. (However, Durkheim did not consider the problem of discontinuities as such, nor were his proposals on discipline intended for a society as flexible and permissive as our own.) More recently, Malinowski has maintained that discontinuity is a necessary condition of individual freedom. Unless the young person is exposed to a variety of different influences producing discontinuities in his growth, his culture is likely to mold him in a single direction. Indeed, in primitive societies the very shock of certain deliberate discontinuities was intended to break the individual's dependence on the attitudes and conduct prescribed for his previous condition in life. Malinowski writes:

. . . at any stage of culture the chances of spiritual freedom, that is, of a variety of points of view and ideological crystallizations, depend, first and foremost, upon the existence of a number of mutually independent institutions, which though related enjoy a considerable degree of autonomy. Indeed, in several educational devices of the primitives, we see that joining a new institution or passing through initiation ceremonies entails a definite attempt to break down the loyalties and interests acquired in earlier life and to introduce new values. The institutions thus each exercise an autonomous spiritual influence on the growing mind.[31]

However, Malinowski does not deal here with the specific problem

---

[30] Cf. *ibid.*, p. 268.
[31] Bronislaw Malinowski, *Freedom and Civilization,* Allen and Unwin, London, 1947, pp. 143–144.

facing the modern adolescent, which is not merely that he is cata-
pulted into a new stage in his life but also that, unlike the primitive youth who passes through carefully prescribed initiation
ceremonies, he has been inadequately prepared for this stage and
is, therefore, at a loss when it arrives.

It may also be argued on behalf of discontinuity that, in order
to grow, one must continually reshape one's attitudes and behavior in the light of fresh experiences. A modern society requires
its members to advance much further from their early experiences
than does a primitive society; hence, a greater measure of culturally induced discontinuity is unavoidable.[32] This argument may
not meet the objection that such discontinuity should be mitigated
as much as possible, but at least it makes this discontinuity far
more comprehensible than it might seem at first glance from the
strictures of Mead and Benedict. Moreover, one might continue
to argue that the experience of discontinuity in his teens helps
a person to handle more drastic shocks and disillusionments later.
A stormy adolescence may well be the prelude to a balanced adulthood.

In general, conservative educators accept discontinuity as inevitable. Believing the school's prime task to be intellectual training, they maintain that it is the responsibility of the family to
teach the child morals and manners and to ease him into the life
of his community. Since most, though by no means all, parents
tend to be more conservative in their values than the school, such
a policy tends to accentuate the gap between the kind of standards
and behavior learned by the child and those finally encountered
in the adult world. Conservatives accept this discontinuity on the
grounds that the moral laxity of many adults does not justify low-
ering the standards taught to the child. However much we may
regret this discontinuity, they say, the way to remove it is not by

---

32 Richard Church, *Language and the Discovery of Reality*, Random House,
New York, 1961, pp. 138–139:

> We are all born into the sphere of primitive experience, with very similar
> (although by no means identical) capacities for learning . . . and our cul-
> tural experience develops our capacities in various ways. The more primi-
> tive culture institutionalizes, stabilizes, and elaborates our earlier forms
> of experience, whereas the more advanced culture tends to transform
> them and replace them with new forms.

debasing the behavior of children but by improving that of adults.

Conservatives also maintain that the child should be taught fixed moral values instead of being allowed to form his own standards. They insist that such values are universal and that, in any case, the child lacks the experience to judge wisely for himself in moral matters. They admit that the inculcation of fixed values implies firmer adult control over children, and, hence, a greater discontinuity between the submissiveness of childhood and the dominance required of maturity. They argue, however, that these values are permanent guides to conduct and do not have to be unlearned at adolescence or at any other time in life. They argue, too, that it is precisely by holding certain fixed values that the child acquires the independence of mind that we expect of the adult instead of conforming to the shifting mores of his peers.

Some conservatives blame some progressivists for contributing to this conformity by teaching the child to imitate adult life before he has learned how to think for himself. As a result, the child grows to maturity not as an independent thinker but as a slave to habits and attitudes that he has absorbed uncritically. As Thomas Molnar has said, "His [the pupil's] pattern of dating, buying, investing, and entertaining are studied and then taught to him so that when he reaches the required age, he may slip into adulthood without noticing it, not as a man with an independent mind but as a prefabricated conformist." [33]

Discontinuity and Intellectual Growth

The best way to minimize discontinuities in intellectual growth is to teach the child as little as possible that he has to unlearn later; and the best way to do this is to teach the child how, not what, to think. This is an end that all contemporary educators would accept; it is over the means that they differ.

Progressivism. In the progressive view, the student should learn how to think chiefly through the scientific study of contemporary

---

[33] Thomas Molnar, *The Future of Education*, Fleet, New York, 1961, p. 63. Molnar, whether he knows it or not, is here not attacking the main body of progressive educators but only a group advocating social adjustment as a prime goal of education.

issues, which he experiences as genuinely problematic to the extent that he is able to relate them to his own interests. It is not so important for him to acquire specific knowledge as it is for him to learn how to apply his intelligence systematically to conditions of life around him. Since in this swiftly changing world a person often lacks definite social canons to guide his choices, the pupil should become accustomed to deriving his principles from whatever material is available rather than relying on received knowledge.

The progressive educator also seeks to close the gap between learning and life. He maintains that, in the primary school especially, the child will comprehend the significance of what he learns only if he understands its application to, and origin in, his own life. This belief follows from the progressive principle that the meaning of an idea lies in the empirical consequences that it implies. Thus, to know something is to be able to predict how it will behave or react in certain situations.[34] It is not enough for the child merely to spell and pronounce words or to read sentences; he must also appreciate the concrete acts and conditions that concepts represent. As John L. Childs points out, "Unless we are to burden the young with meaningless catchphrases—sheer verbalisms—that may deaden their intellectual perceptions and weaken their capacity for thought, we must provide them with the experiences that will communicate the life significance of that which they are expected to learn from oral and printed sources." [35] Clearly, as the child grows older and more capable of abstract thought, he will rely less on primary experiences. Nevertheless, the connection between intellectual training and life itself should remain strong, especially for the less academically gifted pupil.

Some writers on anthropology consider the progressive approach highly appropriate to the unlearning required of the modern child. The pupil must replace previously acquired knowledge by new knowledge if he is to outgrow childlike ways of thought. This is

---

34 John L. Childs, *Education and Morals: An Experimentalist Philosophy of Education*, Appleton-Century-Crofts, New York, 1950, p. 146: "We have the meaning of a thing or a situation, not when we have simply memorized the name by which it is designated, but when we know what to expect of it, how to behave with reference to it, and what can be done with it."
35 *Ibid.*, pp. 146–147.

particularly the case in a swiftly changing culture, where the older child, to adjust properly, may have to study knowledge so recently acquired that it has not been assimilated into the culture's world view and, hence, cannot be taught to the younger child as part of the heritage. Such knowledge cannot simply be added to old knowledge (since, in many cases, it presupposes a different view of reality) but requires that old knowledge be unlearned. Especially is this true of scientific knowledge, which is changing more rapidly than any other and, hence, requires more radical relearning on the part of the student.[36]

This view accords with the progressive principle that learning should be a "transaction," in which the learner interrogates the world, treating it as a vast laboratory in which to test hypotheses. The student can relearn better if he is encouraged to see for himself how this new knowledge improves his conception of the world and enables him to relate to it more effectively. It also tallies with the principle of "learning by doing," in which the student actively tests out what he learns instead of acquiring it by rote and recapitulation.[37]

Conservatism. Conservative educators deny that the child's interests bear any necessary relation either to adult life or to intellectual development. Progressivism, they declare, seeks to maintain continuity between the child's personality and what he learns by making the child's own interests the chief criterion of his studies. Yet, the policy of linking what he learns to his immature inclinations not only discourages him from the full use of his intellectual powers, it actually aggravates the discontinuity that separates him from the adult world.

In this regard, conservatives reject the progressive method of problem solving. The discontinuity created in a modern industrial society between the knowledge and experience of the child and those expected of the adult is not bridged merely by having the child cope with problems of the contemporary culture. If he is to solve problems of a general nature, the pupil must first acquire the habits of orderly thought and a store of knowledge through a

---

36 Cf. Lawrence K. Frank, *The School as Agent for Cultural Renewal,* The Burton Lectures, 1958, Harvard University Press, 1959, pp. 20–21.
37 Cf. *Ibid.,* pp. 27–30.

study of the major intellectual disciplines. These habits of thought do not have to be unlearned, because they represent the tested ways that men have developed to understand and handle certain permanent features of their experience. They form the best preparation for dealing with any culturally induced discontinuity, for they teach a person how to think effectively under all circumstances.

Jerome S. Bruner, an educator with essentialist leanings, has proposed a plan, midway between the conservative and progressive positions, for maintaining continuity in the pupil's intellectual growth.[38] On the premise that "any subject can be taught effectively in some intellectually honest form to any child at any stage of development," Bruner maintains that the elementary school should introduce the child to the basic concepts of the subjects he will study in high school. Since at each stage in his development the child has a characteristic way of thinking, these concepts should be presented in terms that he will appreciate. At present, says Bruner, this is rarely done. For example, in high school the pupil is introduced "cold" to the theorems of Euclidean geometry with no previous experience of simpler geometrical configurations.[39]

According to Bruner, the high school should be able to deepen, refine, add to, and systematize knowledge to which the pupil has already been introduced in simpler terms. He illustrates by referring to the teaching of literature and science. The great forms and the great themes of literature—the forms of tragedy and comedy, for instance, and the themes of identity and personal loyalty—can be taught to the elementary-school child in ways that he will understand. For example, the literature of tragedy can be introduced through such means as the retelling of the great myths, the use of children's classics, and the presentation of and commentary on selected films of proved worth. Later teaching can build on these foundations to create a more explicit and profound un-

---

[38] Jerome S. Bruner, "The Process of Education," in Ronald Gross, ed., *The Teacher and the Taught: The Theory and Practice of Education from Plato to James B. Conant,* Dell, New York, 1963, pp. 248–260.
[39] Bruner mentions the objection that, by introducing pupils to knowledge inductively before teaching it to them formally in the high school, we may perhaps stifle original but unorthodox ideas. He points out that we need factual evidence to settle this question.

derstanding of tragic literature. In science, the pupil should be introduced as early as possible, and in a manner that is both intellectually honest and consistent with his way of thinking, to such general concepts as number, measure, and probability and to the basic notions of the several sciences. These topics, learned at first intuitively and inexactly, can be taught to him with increasing sophistication as he grows older.

In this chapter I have described certain discontinuities, which, in the opinion of anthropologists, our culture has created between the ways of children and the ways of adults. Bridging these discontinuities at adolescence brings on considerable stress and strain. Progressive educators seek to alleviate this stress by reducing the discontinuities. Conservative educators, on the other hand, believe that much discontinuity is inevitable and that the child is best prepared to handle it through the training of his intellectual powers.

7

Education and Cultural Values

VALUES AND CULTURE

A culture's values are its ideals of what is worth striving for. Some of them are precise, such as the value of honesty, whereas others are hard to delineate, like our belief in the supreme worth of the individual. Some, like patriotism, are constantly on men's lips, whereas others, such as the belief that reality can be measured, are rarely acknowledged.

Of the diversity of cultural values there is no doubt.[1] Consider the value of competitiveness, which seems so necessary to the American way of life. Americans are constantly urged to get ahead; our aim is always to win, always to get there first, always to climb one more rung on an endless ladder of prosperity and success. (This is not, of course, to deny that the American is not also pulled by contrary values, such as that of group harmony and cooperation.) Yet, to many primitive peoples competition is abhorrent. Hopi life, for instance, is based on cooperation among men and with nature. A Hopi child is taught never to win a game or to excel his classmates.[2] Among the Mixtecans of Juxtlahuaca, Mexico, envy and competitiveness are minor crimes. A Mixtecan in a position of authority does not give orders to his fellows. If he suggests a course of action, he does so as one dispensing knowledge, not as one dominating others through personality or posi-

---

[1] For an account of how different cultures interpret the notion of equality, see Dorothy Lee, "Equality of Opportunity as a Cultural Value," *Freedom and Culture*, Prentice-Hall, Englewood Cliffs, New Jersey, 1959, pp. 39–52.
[2] See Wayne Dennis, *The Hopi Child*, Appleton-Century, New York, 1940.

tion. Group decisions are the result of consensus rather than majority rule.[3]

Although the values of our culture pervade our lives, they do not mold us alike. For one thing, cultural change is far from symmetrical; hence, conflicting values coexist within the same culture, and different values are affirmed by different individuals. Social groups differ in certain of their values, and, in a pluralist society, especially, a person is exposed to a wide range of such values. Furthermore, each person's private experiences leave their unique imprint on the values of his culture as he sees them.

The average man finds it difficult to regard his values with detachment. In his childhood he learns to regard them as universal and absolute, and, therefore, not to be compromised, for the child cannot understand that something is good unless he is also led to believe that it is good for all men everywhere. The idea, for example, that certain acts, such as lying, may be wrong in general but justified on occasion is too sophisticated for a ten-year-old to grasp. Moreover, having been absorbed for the most part unconsciously in the process of enculturation, these values have entered into the personality of the mature man and have done much to mold it.

Those values acceptable to all members of a culture tend to be very general and, for this reason, difficult to realize fully. Consider some values on which nearly all Americans would agree: that all men should have an equal opportunity to realize their talents; that all men should possess certain rights and freedoms (such as freedom of religion and equality before the law); that problems should be solved rationally and, where appropriate, democratically; and that, if such values are observed, life can be made better for all. But do all Americans really get an equal chance to make something of their lives? Are they all treated alike by the law? And can they be?

THREE ISSUES FOR EDUCATION

Three aspects of the relation of values to culture are particularly

3 See Kimball Romney and Romaine Romney, "The Mixtecans of Juxtlahuaca, Mexico," in Beatrice B. Whiting, ed., *Six Cultures: Studies of Child Rearing*, Wiley, New York, 1963, p. 565.

relevant to the study of anthropology and education. One is the discrepancy between a culture's values and its actual practices— the discrepancy, that is, between ideal and manifest or "actualized" culture. The second is the conflict in values generated by cultural change. The third is the disparity between the dominant values of the culture and the values of minorities within the culture. Let us consider each in turn.

Ideal versus Manifest Culture

The Conflict in Culture. Since no culture is fully integrated, its ideals are bound to vary from its practices. Every culture legitimizes for its members certain goals as well as certain norms (modes of behavior) for attaining them. These norms are not necessarily the most efficient, either for the individual or for the group—most cultures, for instance, prohibit the use of force or fraud to achieve their goals—but they are compatible, as a rule, with the existing values and institutions of the culture. These norms vary, too, in the weight that they carry, for they may be prescribed, preferred, or merely permitted.

Yet, because a culture legitimizes certain norms, it does not follow that they always are observed. The less efficient the norms become as means of reaching the culture's goals, the less the norms tend to be observed. In addition, the more a culture impels its members to concentrate on its goals and the less it emphasizes the norms for attaining them, again the less these norms are observed. The culture thus is threatened by disorganization, until eventually it may reach a state that Durkheim called *anomie,* or normlessness, when the official norms no longer answer to the realities of life in the culture.[4]

In America certain success goals, especially those connected

---

[4] Robert K. Merton, "Social Structure and Anomie," *Social Theory and Social Structure,* The Free Press of Glencoe, New York, 1957, p. 135:

> With such differential emphases upon goals and institutional procedures, the latter may be so vitiated by the stress on goals as to have the behavior of many individuals limited only by considerations of technical experience. In this context, the sole significant question becomes: Which of the available procedures is most efficient in netting the culturally approved value?

with wealth and its symbols (the summer home, the winter cruise, the private airplane), are acclaimed far more emphatically than the institutionalized means for attaining them. Our culture insists that, if a man works hard and overtime, he will succeed in life— that is, he will make a lot of money. Yet, only a few men can get rich by working long and hard, for "rich" is a relative term and the rich, by definition, must necessarily be few. (In a country of millionaires only billionaires are wealthy.) This is not to mention such other barriers to success as social class and racial or ethnic origin, which may not make hard work futile but considerably limit the benefits to be gained by it. Thus, despite the fact that the culturally sanctioned norm of hard work rarely leads to the wealth it is supposed to, all men are urged, nevertheless, to strive for success as the culture defines it. The result may be not only anxiety or frustration but also antisocial behavior, as men seek more effective ways than the official norms to gratify the success drives implanted in them.

Of itself, lack of opportunity does not cause deviant behavior; it is the combination of inadequate opportunity and the acclamation of success goals not for a few but for the whole population. The culture holds out certain goals for all its members, yet the conditions of culture render the approved means of reaching these goals ineffective for most people. The culture, in short, arouses expectations that can rarely be fulfilled in the ways it provides.

Let me mention a few more discrepancies between the theory and practice of American culture. On the one hand, we extol free enterprise. On the other, a few large firms dominate the economy; broad sectors of this economy, such as defense and aviation, are financed by the Federal government; and the small, independent businessman, praised in the chambers of commerce, is crushed by the economics of mass production. Again, individualism is prized but togetherness is practiced. In addition, youngsters are encouraged to date early and marry late, yet premarital intercourse is frowned upon. Then, as I stated earlier, there is the popular disdain of the teacher, who is "too theoretical" and insufficiently "practical," but who, nevertheless, becomes suspect if he enters the arena of politics or the marketplace of industry and commerce.

The Conflict in Education. In a thousand and one ways American schools transmit and reinforce the values of their culture. Since most teachers and administrators come from the middle class, much educational practice reflects, however covertly, middle-class attitudes.[5] Although schoolmen differ in many respects, all nevertheless embody certain values, such as the importance of adult authority, the need for order and discipline, the value of knowledge and of educational achievement, and such middle-class traits as neatness, politeness, correct speech, and respect for property. The culture's values are also subtly manifested in the school curriculum. Courses in civics convey the values of an open democracy, collective action, and the possibility of improving the human lot. Courses in history tend to depict the culture in a favorable light.[6]

A school's activities and organization also convey accepted values.[7] In the classroom the child learns to be punctual, write legibly, use paper sparingly, and be quiet when the teacher is speaking. Raising his hand to make suggestions and answer questions reinforces the drive to compete and excel. In games he learns to play fair and to take his turn with others. In clubs he learns the prestige of being an officer. From school festivities he acquires loyalty to his school and solidarity with fellow students. Nevertheless, being exposed to these values does not guarantee that he absorbs them as his own; other factors interfere, such as the special norms of the peer group, the unpopularity of certain teachers, and perhaps parental apathy toward his education.

Inevitably, the school finds itself caught in the conflict between ideal and manifest culture. Should it educate the child in the direc-

---

[5] Robert J. Havighurst, "Social Class and the American School System," in George Z. F. Bereday and Luigi Volpicelli, eds., *Public Education in America: A New Interpretation of Purpose and Practice,* Harper, New York, 1958, p. 86:

> They [teachers] attempt to serve as trustees of the educational system in the interests of the entire society *as they understand these interests.* This means that they tend to favor the teaching of middle class skills and attitudes in the schools, and that they favor types of education which promote social mobility.

[6] Cf. Penelope Leach, "Teaching Tolerance," *International Review of Education,* X, 2, 1964, pp. 196–197.

[7] Cf. Frederick Elkins, *The Child and Society: The Process of Socialization,* Random House, New York, 1958, pp. 59–60.

tion of certain theoretically desirable objectives or should it condition him to the existing realities of the culture? According to the democratic ethos, people should cooperate to get things done, but in most of our society they compete. Hence, the school oscillates between encouraging children to cooperate and encouraging them to compete, and does not take a firm stand for either value. We extol the idea that everyone should have an equal opportunity to pursue the career most suited to his talents, yet, in most careers, it is disproportionately difficult for a woman to succeed. As a result, the school wavers between encouraging girls to become the career women that officially they are entitled to be and training them to be the housewives most of them become. There is also the discrepancy between the belief that education should liberate the mind of every student, no matter what his background, and the fact that colleges are selective in their admission policies. Hence, the school swings between educating for intellectual development and educating for adjustment to further schooling.

Perhaps the greatest gulf is between the ideal of equality and the fact of segregation. Not only are many schools and social institutions segregated still, but even in the greater part of the country where segregation officially does not exist, it is difficult for a Negro student to get as good an education as a white student, partly because schools in Negro neighborhoods tend to be poorly staffed and poorly administered, partly because the predominantly white schools are pervaded by white attitudes to which the Negro student is unaccustomed. Other ethnic minorities, such as Mexicans and Puerto Ricans, are in a similar plight.[8]

Traditional versus Emergent Values

The Conflict in Culture. As a culture changes—from, say, agrarianism to industrialism—either some or all of its values will change or become reinterpreted, although not necessarily together or immediately. The transformation of the United States into an affluent society has juxtaposed the values of the Puritan ethic with those of an industrial society geared to abundance. In order to

---

[8] Cf. Ruth Landes, "Culture and Education," in George F. Kneller, ed., *Foundations of Education*, Wiley, New York, 1963, pp. 320–352.

provide for its own growth, business must constantly persuade people to consume ever larger quantities of nonessentials. As a result, abstinence is retreating before consumption, thrift before installment buying.[9] Sexuality, once the prime example of abstinence, is being stimulated more and more by dress, advertising, and mass entertainment. Belief in the importance of the future is yielding to the view that the present should be enjoyed since the future is uncertain. Self-reliance is giving way to group-mindedness.

Some critics, it is true, deny that the nucleus of the American value system has changed at all. This nucleus, say Talcott Parsons and Winston White, is the concept of "instrumental individualism," or the belief that a person should aim at the kinds of success that benefit his society.[10] Today, they maintain, a person is still expected to work hard and not relax until he has achieved success. What has changed are the specific ends to be achieved and the means for achieving them. At one time, the goal was monetary profit by means of investment, and the type was the entrepreneur. Now the goal is high competence in a specialized role within a large organization, a goal attained by performing the role responsibly in order to meet approval. The type is the flexible, other-directed executive. Nevertheless, whether the values emerging from the social and economic changes of the twentieth century are replacing fundamental American values or merely reinterpreting them, the fact remains that these values exist and are at odds with the values—or interpretations—emphasized formerly.

The Conflict in Education. The conflict between traditional and emergent values frequently manifests itself in a discrepancy between the intent and the actual effect of teaching, between the effect the teacher wishes to have, and probably thinks he has, and

---

[9] Cf. George Dearborn Spindler, *The Transmission of American Culture,* The Burton Lectures, 1957, Harvard University Press, 1959, p. 6, and "Education in a Transforming American Culture," in George D. Spindler, ed., *Education and Culture: Anthropological Approaches,* Holt, Rinehart and Winston, New York, 1963, pp. 136–137.

[10] Talcott Parsons and Winston White, "The Link Between Character and Society," in Seymour Martin Lipset and Leo Lowenthal, eds., *Culture and Social Character: The Work of David Riesman Reviewed,* The Free Press of Glencoe, New York, 1961, pp. 89–133.

the effect he actually does have.[11] In Spindler's view, educators tend on the whole to be less traditional in their values than the general public.[12] Young teachers especially lean most strongly toward emergent values, followed by older teachers and then by administrators. School boards tend to be the most conservative, since they generally consist of older members of the community who have succeeded in life and, therefore, tend to support the values of the established order. Students may be more or less conservative than their teachers, depending to some extent on whether the value orientation of their families is traditional or emergent. If it is traditional, children will tend to hold traditional values less firmly than their parents; if emergent, they will tend to embrace emergent values more wholeheartedly. On the other hand, children may also take up extreme traditional or emergent positions as part of a rebellion against their parents or adults in general.

Having experienced and, to some extent, internalized these cultural conflicts, teachers, as cultural transmitters, tend to pass them on to their students, thereby frustrating or obscuring many intended goals of education. As a rule they do not transmit these conflicts deliberately but rather reflect unconsciously the state of contemporary culture. Indeed, these conflicts permeate the whole subculture of education, most obviously in the design of curricula, in methods of teaching, in textbooks and teaching aids, in student-teacher relations, and in the professional training of teachers.

Consider some examples. Social studies are designed to acquaint the student, among other things, with the theory and practice of American democracy; yet frequently, in the name of doing things democratically in the classroom, they fail to train the capacity for independent, abstract thought, which democracy also needs. They

---

[11] Of course, not all such discrepancies are the result of a conflict in cultural values. The pupil may simply not respond in the way the teacher anticipates. Cf. Jules Henry's discussion of three kinds of attitudes, "indeterminate," "antithetical," and "pseudo-complementary," which the teacher may arouse unconsciously: "A Cross-Cultural Survey of Education," *Current Anthropology*, I, No. 4 (July 1960), 301–302.

[12] George D. Spindler, "Education in a Transforming American Culture," in George D. Spindler, ed., *Education and Culture: Anthropological Approaches*, Holt, Rinehart and Winston, New York, pp. 139–141. See also his *The Transmission of American Culture*, The Burton Lecture, 1957, Harvard, 1959.

tend, moreover, to reinforce those habits of group behavior already firmly embedded in the emergent value pattern.

Textbooks, too, often communicate unintended meanings. Dorothy Lee has examined one home economics textbook and fifteen state and city manuals in use in elementary and secondary schools. She mentions a number of discrepancies.[13] One book declares that it seeks to help the student "share meaningful experiences in the home." Although it provides a host of details on various household activities, such as choosing recipes, finishing seams, and doing laundry, it says nothing about the people who share these activities or who are being helped. Another books states that its goal is to help the student to enjoy the home "creatively" and to "appreciate" family living, yet it treats housework as something to be done as efficiently as possible, so that one can have more leisure time away from it. Another states that it seeks to develop a mature personality (which one would suppose called for some attention to the life of the intellect and the imagination), yet it emphasizes the external traits, congenial to the other-directed personality, of grooming, manners, popularity, making friends, and using one's time efficiently. All these textbooks, then, contain matter that is at odds with their declared goals.

Turning to classroom procedures, we find that many teachers seek to transmit the cultural heritage by permissive methods that produce a degree of freedom at variance with the attentiveness the teachers need if they are to communicate the heritage effectively. Jules Henry, for instance, describes elementary-school teachers who unconsciously transmit the cultural phenomenon of "intragroup aggression."[14] Here the group turns on its own members, who do not resist this aggression in the manner of the inner-directed individualist but rather learn to live with it. He cites a fifth-grade teacher who devoted one period to hearing short reports, which members of the class were asked to criticize. The teacher intended the experience to develop skill in writing and

---

[13] Dorothy Lee, "Discrepancies in the Teaching of American Culture," in George D. Spindler, ed., *Education and Culture: Anthropological Approaches,* Holt, Rinehart and Winston, New York, 1963, pp. 173–191.

[14] Jules Henry, "Attitude Organization in Elementary School Classrooms," *American Journal of Orthopsychiatry,* XXVII (January 1957), 117–133.

reporting and, one presumes, to help students to learn from criticism. In fact, however, no constructive criticism was forthcoming; nor did the teacher seek it out. As a result, and quite contrary to the teacher's intention, the children indulged in destructive criticism of one another's work, and the habit of intragroup aggression, already partly internalized from the culture, was reinforced. Furthermore, in their relations with students many teachers seek to be leaders and counselors; but in order to do this, they often curry student favor and affection to such an extent that they can no longer maintain discipline.

Inheriting, as a rule, the traditional values of the middle or lower-middle class, the prospective teacher enters the subculture of a training institution whose values are generally emergent. This institution tends to regard the prime end of education as enabling the child to work and play harmoniously with the other members of his group—often to the deteriment of individual growth. The future teacher is thus in a position similar to that of an acculturating population, which somehow must handle the conflict between its own culture and the new culture that it is increasingly accepting.

The teacher may react in a number of ways. If he feels threatened by the new values, he may reaffirm his old values the more emphatically and project them uncomprisingly in the classroom. He may also overcompensate in the opposite direction by accepting the new values uncritically and seeking group harmony at all costs. If he is not given to introspection. he may internalize both sides of the conflict unconsciously without synthesizing them into a consistent value pattern of his own. In the latter case he will oscillate between different methods of handling groups and individuals and, through his inconsistencies, will make trouble for himself and his pupils. Finally, if he is thoughtful and stable, he may acknowledge the conflict but not feel threatened by it, in which case he will synthesize elements of both patterns into a coherent system of his own. In the classroom he will follow a *via media* between extreme individualism and extreme groupism. Spindler believes that this type of teacher is becoming more numerous although unfortunately he is still in a minority.[15]

---

[15] George Dearborn Spindler, *The Transmission of American Culture,* The Burton Lecture, 1957, Harvard University Press, 1959, pp. 27–28.

In Spindler's view the first two types of teacher transmit too narrowly; the former because, contrary to his declared knowledge and intentions, he communicates effectively only with middle-class children who share his values; the latter because he aims at a group harmony that pays little attention to individuals. Both teachers may stimulate a few children, but they will fail to influence the majority. The third type communicates to many children in many ways, but is too weak and too inconsistent to transmit the culture effectively. The fourth teacher, on the other hand, having consciously synthesized the best elements of both value patterns, is able to reach more children in more ways; hence, he "transmits along many channels."

To tackle the problem of unconsciously transmitted cultural conflicts, Spindler recommends what he calls "cultural therapy." [16] In a few cases the cultural therapist can study the teacher privately and in his classroom and, by showing him how internalized values are narrowing his attitudes, can help him to deepen and broaden his approach. However, since this operation consumes much time and energy, Spindler suggests that the information gained in these cases should be put at the disposal of student teachers in foundations courses in order to help them examine their internalized values before the classroom calls these values into action.

But here a dilemma arises, for the cultural conflicts transmitted to children in the school are also beneficial in that they contribute to variations in personalities and, hence, to cultural innovation. One solution is for the teacher to acknowledge these conflicts more explicitly, even in the act of transmitting them, or, better, to transmit only selected conflicts. But there is a danger here too, for if we can control the conflicts that we transmit, we will be prone to transmit the culture too narrowly and, hence, to induce conformity. Suppose, on the other hand, that the teacher seeks to be eclectic and thereby to stimulate as many children as possible. Can he at the same time transmit the cultural heritage effectively to each of these children? We are left, then, with a theoretical problem which educators have still to solve: In order to encourage individual differences and, at the same time, avoid unconscious conflict in the student, teachers must know and control the conflicts

---

[16] *Ibid.*, p. 49.

they transmit; yet, if they can do this, they are in a position to induce an undesirable conformity.

Dominant versus Minority Values

The Conflict in Culture. Many Americans live outside the dominant American culture, which is roughly that of the middle class.[17] They have not been brought up in it, and they do not aspire to it. Many of them are separated from it by poverty and many by race, and a high proportion are undereducated.[18] Since education has done little for them, many have little faith in what it can do for their children; and those who are eager to have their children well educated can give them little help, since they lack formal schooling themselves. This alienation from the majority culture is especially severe among those of non-European ancestry, of whom I shall consider the Mexican American and the American Negro in particular.[19]

Except that both belong to subcultures, Negroes and Mexicans have little in common. Traditionally, the Negro has been closer than the Mexican to the life around him, and his culture more

---

[17] A considerable proportion belong to the "forgotten fifth" of the nation who live below the poverty line. In 1962 thirty million Americans lived in families with annual incomes of under $3,000—less than $60 a week. Five million more unattached Americans had annual incomes of less than $1,500 a year. Of the poor families 47 per cent lived in the South, 25 per cent in the North Central region, 17 per cent in the Northeast, and 11 per cent in the West. Nearly half of all nonwhite Americans live in poverty. *New York Times,* January 21, 1964.

[18] About six out of ten heads of families in the poverty group have had eight years of school or less. Expressed differently, nearly 40 per cent of heads of families with no more than eighth-grade education belong to the poverty group, whereas fewer than 10 per cent of those with more than a high-school education belong to this group. *New York Times,* January 9, 1964.

[19] Since my concern in this book is with cultural, rather than physical, anthropology, I consider race here as a social and cultural, not as a genetic, phenomenon. Whether the Negro's present cultural deficiencies are genetically as well as environmentally conditioned is an area of controversy that I cannot enter. See correspondence to *Science,* CXLII (13 December 1963), 1419–1420, and CXLIII (24 January 1964), 306–308.

clearly reflects the dominant American values. The Mexican tends to hold himself aloof. Under discrimination, against which the Negro may protest, the Mexican withdraws, often covering his retreat with politeness. The Mexican tends not to attend school conferences and PTA meetings. When the school asks him to cooperate in seeing that his son arrives on time or that his daughter does her homework, he often replies that he *intends* to do so. Politeness and procrastination are his way of avoiding conflict.[20]

Mexican culture, writes Ruth Landes, is more authoritarian than Negro culture. Unlike most other American children, white and Negro, Mexican children are expected to wait for adult direction, usually that of parents or elder siblings, rather than to exercise their own initiative. Hence, writes Landes, if they are to behave with initiative in the schools, they must be taught how to set aside their traditional habits of deference. Their teachers, too, must handle them more firmly than they would other American children. School counselors must expect to make more decisions for them. School officers must follow up their decisions by seeing parents personally and getting in touch with them by letter and phone—ways that other Americans would find interfering and even overbearing.[21]

The Negro woman, continues Landes, enjoys a freedom similar to that of the white woman. Negro parents are not surprised when their children are taught by women teachers and follow certain dating habits actually encouraged by the school. Mexican women, on the other hand, especially if young and unmarried, are not expected to hold positions of authority. Hence, Mexican parents are often disconcerted when their older children are instructed by young, unmarried female teachers and affronted when their daughters acquire some of the sexual independence of the normal American girl.[22]

A child of the white middle class tends to bring to his school a very different outlook from that of the lower-class child, white or colored. From infancy on he has been more carefully fed,

---

[20] Ruth Landes, "Culture and Education," in George F. Kneller, ed., *Foundations of Education*, Wiley, New York, 1963, p. 328.
[21] *Ibid.*, pp. 341–342.
[22] *Ibid.*, pp. 332–333, 345. However, in urban communities in Mexico this is ceasing to be true (author).

clothed, and guarded by parents who have the time and money to spend on him. Tenderness and understanding, pride and affection, have been shown him from the beginning. He is confident and at ease in a world in which he assumes that he will succeed as a matter of course. Having absorbed the drive and directedness of his parents, he is purposeful and self-confident.

The children of the poor have rarely known such solicitude. Their parents have not had time to give it to them—the father physically tired and perhaps chronically unemployed, the mother at work or overburdened with household chores. The world of the white middle class is indifferent to them, perhaps even hostile. Having little to aim for, they lack ambition; they feel alienated from the wider society; and they have little sense of purpose. Mexicans excepted, they are less disciplined, especially sexually, than middle-class children and express themselves more forcibly and brusquely. Instead of restraining their inclinations in order to strive for future goals, they tend to live for the moment.

The Conflict in Education. The typical American school is imbued with middle-class values. It expects children to be polite, to follow the conventions, and to respect other people's property. It encourages hard work, sportsmanship, and, above all, ambition. To all these values the middle-class child is already accustomed. His teachers, members of the middle class themselves, respond to him with understanding and appreciation. But to the lower-class child many of these values are alien. He does not feel himself a part of the school, because the values of the school are not his. Hence, talented lower-class children rarely do so well in school as middle-class children of equal and even lesser ability, and some of them drop out even when they are intellectually capable of continuing.[23]

The school's middle-class culture sets the lower-class child at

---

[23] In one study Robert J. Havighurst found that for every high-school dropout from the upper and upper-middle classes there were about 32 from the upper-lower and lower-lower classes. Moreover, fifteen students entered college from the two top social classes for every one from the two lower classes. Havighurst also found that, when the proportion of middle-class children in a school approached or fell below 40 per cent, their parents began either to leave the neighborhood or to enroll their children in private schools, Robert J. Havighurst et al., *Growing Up in River City*, Wiley, New York, 1962, pp. 50–53.

a disadvantage in innumerable ways. The language of the school is unfamiliar to him. His textbooks, too, appeal to middle-class attitudes, especially that of ambition, and their illustrations often depict middle-class people in middle-class situations. He is not at ease with his teachers, who dress, talk, and think differently and appreciate different things. The subjects that he studies—grammar, history, and science—seem to him to have little or no bearing on the sordid and sometimes desperate circumstances with which he must cope when out of school. The very procedures of the school may violate the canons to which he is accustomed.[24]

How are educators to surmount the cultural differences that hinder effective communication? First, in order to understand the expectations that children bring to school, educators must study the cultures in which the children are reared. They must use this knowledge to develop appropriate techniques for all aspects of the educational process. They will find that many problems spring not from the fractiousness of the pupil or his parents, but rather from the latters' misinterpretation of ways of speech and action to which they are unaccustomed. Ruth Landes tells the case of an intelligent but unruly Korean-American boy who was nearly excluded from his school because the school authorities did not comprehend the cultural traditions of his Korean father. Unaware of the veneration accorded by Koreans to the head of the household, school representatives tried persistently to reach the mother. Finally, when the father was approached in the manner to which he was accustomed, he cooperated with the school in controlling the child.[25]

The teacher must also examine the influence of culture on his own behavior. Unless he knows the cultural signals that he himself is sending out, he gains little from perceiving the signals of his pupils. Ideally, this self-examination should be carried out dur-

---

[24] For instance, in the 1930's Otto Klineberg discovered that some children of the Plains Indians had failed in the Indian schools because they would not act competitively in the way their white teachers wanted them to. Although each child was expected to recite publicly and be praised for his display of knowledge, none did so because this was felt to be boastful and a public shaming of one's kinsmen. See Otto Klineberg, *Race Differences,* Harper, New York, 1935 and later editions, quoted by Ruth Landes "Culture and Education," in George F. Kneller, ed., *Foundations of Education,* Wiley, New York, 1963, p. 324.

[25] *Ibid.,* p. 330.

ing his training, although to the thoughtful, actual teaching experience will be the great enlightener.[26]

Since he feels alienated from the wider society, the lower-class child, and especially the minority child, often lacks the drive to aim at vocational goals that he is otherwise capable of attaining. It should, therefore, be the responsibility of the school counselor to foster vocational ambitions receiving little or no encouragement from parents, community, or peers.[27] He should provide an example of successful male adulthood, which the lower-class boy can imitate and, in so doing, develop long-term ambitions of his own as well as the personality traits needed to attain them. Other means of encouraging ambition, both academic and vocational, are to increase the scholarship aid offered by institutions of higher education, to acquaint the student with examples of successful professional persons from his own racial, ethnic, or class background, and to encourage parents to sympathize with the newly awakened ambitions of their children.

If the school can interest parents in their children's education, it has gone a long way toward overcoming cultural differences.[28]

---

[26] *Ibid.*, pp. 336–340. According to Landes, teachers of Mexican and Puerto Rican children should, if possible, learn Spanish. Although, clearly, these students must master English, they should not be penalized for reverting to their own language, particularly in conversation among themselves. If they are to retain the pride in self to which they are entitled and which is necessary for effective learning, their language must be treated with the respect it deserves and not as an inferior argot used to deceive or shut out their teachers. A command of Spanish can win for a teacher the affection and trust of pupils on whom other teachers have little influence.

[27] Cf. David P. Ausubel, "A Teaching Strategy for Culturally Deprived Pupils: Cognitive and Motivational Considerations," *The School Review*, Winter, 1963, 462–463.

[28] Cf. Clemmont E. Vontress, "Our Demoralizing Slum Schools," *Phi Delta Kappan*, XLV, No. 2 (November 1963), 81. Vontress says that if parents do not respond to the school's invitations, the school must move its activities into the neighborhood, setting up "Education Appreciation" workshops in whatever halls they can find. See also Frederick Shaw, "Educating Culturally Deprived Youth in Urban Centers," *ibid.*, 93. In addition to winning the support of parents, Shaw maintains that the school should seek the backing of the whole community. To do so, it may set up programs of activities for youth in the afternoons and for adults in the evenings. It may also enlist the help of other public and private agencies, such as libraries, neighborhood service organizations, YMCA's and YWCA's. In serving the needs of the

Teachers and administrators must gain the confidence of parents who regard the school as merely another alien power determining their lives. To this end, the school should offer parents courses in such practical subjects as speech, shorthand, typing, sewing, and millinery, as well as refresher courses in reading, arithmetic, and such other academic subjects as will enable them to help their children in school work. It should also encourage them to take courses in budgeting, food preparation, furniture repair, household tasks, and family relations generally.

CULTURAL VALUES AND EDUCATIONAL THOUGHT

Progressivism

Let us turn finally to the views of educational theorists on the question whether or not the school should promote certain of the culture's values. The progressive educator maintains that since all circumstances and societies change and since there is no permanent human nature, all values are necessarily provisional. Right action consists less in adherence to fixed standards than in action based on reflection. The student, then, should learn not values as such, but rather how to discover them through reflective thinking. He should not be conditioned to apply a fixed code of conduct to the varied and elastic circumstances of life; rather he should learn to appraise in advance the probable consequences to himself and to others of the alternative courses of action available to him in particular situations. The teacher should propose the traditional values of Western culture as hypotheses—good ones, to be sure, since they have long served to adjust men to circumstances and to one another, but as hypotheses nevertheless—which the student should test to see whether they help him to solve his present problems.[29]

The progressive educator believes that in a pluralist democracy

whole community the school contributes visibly and positively to the lives of the adults and youngsters whose attitude to education materially influences the behavior of the school's students.

[29] George R. Geiger, "An Experimentalist Approach to Education," in Nelson B. Henry, ed., *Modern Philosophies and Education*, The Fifty-fourth Yearbook of the National Society for the Study of Education, University of Chicago Press, 1955, p. 161.

the school cannot rightly dictate what the student's hierarchy of values should be. Nevertheless, it can influence the student's choice of values by inviting him to consider certain values rather than others as part of his general education. To insure that all students share the common experience of getting to grips with these values in a contemporary setting, the teacher must use a wide variety of methods and materials. Otherwise, given, say, a single book to read, each student will simply seize on the ideas that meet his particular interest instead of sharing the same general experience with his fellows.[30]

In any other-directed culture, social and cultural change is liable to get out of hand, since people lack firm values for assessing which changes are desirable and which are not. Few progressives any longer maintain that stability can be found in the process of change itself. In order, then, to find his own hierarchy of values, the student must be taught how to examine the values motivating much contemporary behavior, so that he will not accept the behavior of those around him without assessing its assumptions and consequences. He must study various aspects and problems of the contemporary culture, such as advertising, the automobile, and divorce, in order to understand the values that they imply and to judge them for himself. By studying current behavior and artifacts rather than abstract or historical issues, he is better able to work out for himself a realistic hierarchy of values relevant to the world he must live in.[31]

Conservatism

The conservative view of values in education takes two forms, the *perennialist* and the *essentialist*. Perennialists, believing in an

---

[30] Cf. Harold L. Hodgkinson, *Education in Social and Cultural Perspectives,* Prentice-Hall, Englewood Cliffs, New Jersey, 1962, pp. 133–134.

[31] *Ibid.,* p. 138. Hodgkinson mentions the case of some school children in Hagerstown, Maryland, who were given constant practice during school hours in watching television critically, with the result that they became much more selective in the programs they watched out of school. He writes:

> Here the school has *unintentionally* built into many students a hierarchy of values which allows them to be selective instead of being inundated by a steady flow of one program after another. If it can be done unintentionally, why could not the school intentionally develop a program to promote sophistication in analysis of a wide range of social behaviors?

absolute hierarchy of values, maintain that, contrary to present practice, it is the school's duty to inculcate these values. In Hutchins' words:

The prime object of education is to know what is good for man. It is to know the goods in their order. There is a hierarchy of values. The task of education is to help us understand it, establish it, and live by it.[32]

The essentialist view is that although the school should not give overt moral training, nevertheless, in developing the intellect it is cultivating the important moral values of intellectual honesty and reflective thinking. The school should also influence the moral character of its students by insuring that its own activities are conducted according to moral standards that the students clearly understand. Thus, it should encourage students to be honest in their work; it should reward them according to actual performance; and it should give high prestige to serious intellectual activities. Harry Broudy states that the school gives moral education when it encourages devotion to truth and reason, assists the pupil to use his talents to the full, and initiates self-knowledge by making the student think about himself and personally test his own abilities.[33]

The conservative point of view is also defended by I. B. Berkson, who rejects the progressive contention that the child should be allowed to form his own hierarchy of values. The school, he says, should teach the values of Western culture, which are more reliable than the judgments of a student.[34] He also criticizes the progressive attempt to train the character by imitating situations in real life. He points out that the main moral issues of adult life, such as those concerned with marriage or one's career, are too complex for the school to duplicate at all adequately. Instead, the school should train the character in two ways: by teaching the child contemporary mores, thereby producing social stability, and by teaching him the enduring ideals of the culture, thereby en-

---

[32] Robert M. Hutchins, *The Conflict in Education in a Democratic Society,* Harper, New York, 1953, p. 71.
[33] Harry S. Broudy, *Building a Philosophy of Education,* Prentice-Hall, Englewood Cliffs, New Jersey, 1961, p. 241.
[34] I. B. Berkson, *The Ideal and the Community: A Philosophy of Education,* Harper, New York, 1958, p. 244.

abling him to criticize and improve these mores when he is an adult.[35]

Both types of conservatism maintain that it is the parents' responsibility to teach the child certain values that he later may assess for himself. To bring him up without fixed standards is not to emancipate but to confuse him. Meanwhile, the school should give him the intellectual training he needs if he is to weigh these values objectively in later life. Although parents should not pretend for the child's sake to hold values in which they do not believe, it is still their responsibility to instill those in which they do believe. As one child psychologist puts it:

Deliberate attempts to bring up the child in an atmosphere of relativism are probably misguided. For reasons of moral, emotional, and intellectual growth—insofar as these can be separated—it probably works better to hold children to a stable set of standards, meanwhile giving them an education that will enable them, later on, to work out a personal orientation.[36]

In this chapter I have examined the influence of our culture's values on its educational system. To this end I have considered three main topics: the discrepancy between ideal and manifest culture, the conflict in values brought about by cultural change, and the disparity between dominant and minority cultural values. In order to help the student and future teacher to decide for himself how to promote his chosen values, I have concluded by reviewing the opinions of leading educational theorists on the desirability of inculcating values in the school.

---

[35] Ibid.
[36] Richard Church, Language and the Discovery of Reality, Random House, New York, 1961, p. 141.

8

Curriculum and Teacher
in Cultural Perspective

THE CURRICULUM IN CONTEMPORARY CULTURE

Three facts of contemporary American culture raise important issues for the curriculum. First, since this culture changes so swiftly, what sorts of subjects will best prepare people to live their lives in a world of continuous change? Second, as this culture grows ever more complex, how are institutions of education to teach the increasingly specialized knowledge and skills that the culture requires and yet maintain the continuity of the heritage? Finally, since many Americans are born with limited access to the dominant middle class culture, how are we to educate them to participate more fully in the wider culture?

Curriculum for a Changing Culture

The Problem. In a stable culture knowledge, as a rule, is transmitted "vertically" from the older members of society to the younger. Even in a culture as dynamic as our own, formal education is largely of this pattern, being the transmission of tried and tested knowledge by old, experienced teachers to young, inexperienced pupils. Yet, as change quickens, new knowledge, whether in the laboratory or on the assembly line, must be transferred with increasing speed.[1] As a result, more and more knowledge is being transmitted "laterally" from the informed to the uninformed, regardless of age. Children, for example, tell their grandparents about the exploration of space or show them how to handle television. Young technicians explain new equipment to old hands. Young scientists achieve breakthroughs that aid their seniors in their research.

Modern man must learn continuously, for new knowledge unceasingly alters his life. Production and consumption, for example, constantly require new learning. A technician must install a new machine; the factory supervisor must introduce it to the staff; the union representative must explain it to the men; the foreman must see that the men operate it. Advertiser and salesman must find markets for the product of this machine. The serviceman must learn to service the product, the housewife to use it, and the mother to answer questions about it from a curious child. As time passes, the cycle of discovery followed by learning is increasingly frequent and increasingly rapid.

Most Americans cease to be educated formally at the age of eighteen, yet this education is expected to suffice them for the rest of their lives. In a relatively static culture educators can assume that the needs and conditions of society will not change too radically in a lifetime. But who can predict the needs and conditions of America half a century hence? [2] As the rate of cultural change accelerates, educators find it increasingly difficult to adapt the curriculum to the so-called demands of society, since they do not know exactly what these demands are or how long they will last. Moreover, curricula cannot be altered overnight; in a democratic society, especially, every proposed modification has to be debated. Nor can they be altered too much, since too radical a change would undermine the continuity between age groups brought up under different courses of study.

---

[1] Cf. Margaret Mead, "Why Is Education Obsolescent?" in Ronald Gross, ed., *The Teacher and the Taught: Education in Theory and Practice from Plato to James B. Conant*, Dell, New York, 1963, pp. 262, 272.

[2] The past two decades have given rise to more new knowledge than the whole history of civilization before the twentieth century. Virgil A. Clift, "Factors Relating to the Education of Culturally Deprived Negro Youth," *Educational Theory*, XIV, No. 2 (April 1964), 78–79.

Today, one of the main forces driving cultural and, hence, curricular change is science and its application in technology. As science improves our knowledge and mastery of the physical world, it also challenges established values and constantly adds to the vast accumulation of facts which we must take into account in order to act. Through technology science influences the economy, creating new jobs and destroying old ones, and it promises with automation to transform the whole pattern of employment.[3] Through technology, too, as in transport and communications, science influences social arrangements, bringing the world closer together and everywhere spreading urbanism and industry.

Science and technology lead also to an increasing specialization of knowledge and function, in education as elsewhere. There are other changes, too, but most have either sprung from science and technology or been influenced by them: a growing population, increased leisure, greater affluence, fresh forms of entertainment, an expansion in the power and responsibility of governments, new methods of warfare and diplomacy (largely created by the discovery and development of nuclear power), and the growing interdependence of nations. All these factors make one thing clear: The school today must educate its pupils so that they can adapt to the unforeseeable events that are bound to occur in their lifetimes. As Margaret Mead has said, "No one will live all his life in the world into which he was born, and no one will die in the world in which he worked in his maturity."[4]

---

[3] At present most Americans are working in commerce and manufacturing, whereas only 12 per cent are employed in agriculture. More now are in the professions and in the management of commerce and industry—8 per cent of the labor force in 1850, 19 per cent a century later—thereby increasing the proportion of the upper-middle class to the population as a whole. See Robert J. Havighurst, "Social Class and the American School System," in George Z. F. Bereday and Luigi Volpicelli, eds., *Public Education in America: A New Interpretation of Purpose and Practice*, Harper, New York, 1958, pp. 82–83.

[4] Margaret Mead, "Why is Education Obsolescent?" in Ronald Gross, ed., *The Teacher and The Taught: Education in Theory and Practice from Plato to James B. Conant*, Dell, New York, 1963, pp. 262–276. In this essay Mead advances one of the more sweeping proposals that have been made for adapting education to rapid cultural change. She advocates a radical division of primary and secondary education. Primary education, she says, should be universal. It should comprise the fundamental skills of reading, writing, and

The Progressive Solution. Progressive educators maintain that in order to adapt American education to an era of rapid change, we must focus both general and special curricula on the contemporary culture.[5] From general studies the student should receive the intellectual training and foundational knowledge he needs to understand present and future changes. If he sees these changes against the broad background of the culture, he will comprehend them better, for to understand change is largely to see it in perspective. From the general curriculum, too, he should acquire a hierarchy of values—not absolute, but rather open to revision—in terms of which he can decide whether to welcome, accept, or reject specific changes. For example, he should form his own standards of public and private morality, so that he can judge intelligently changing standards in such matters as divorce, birth control, and racial integration.[6]

If, therefore, both kinds of curricula deal with the contemporary culture but from different points of view, the student will learn

---

arithmetic and a basic knowledge of the world in which the child is growing up, to include money, geography, transportation, communication, and law. Then, instead of requiring all young people to receive a similar secondary education between the same ages, we should permit each person to acquire as much secondary education as he likes when he likes. Those who wish to leave school early should be allowed to do so, and the firms they join should permit them to resume their education later. This procedure would relieve the high school of many youngsters who have no wish to study further at this stage and whose presence only hinders those who do. It would also permit people to change careers far more easily, because it would enable them to reeducate themselves for a second or third occupation. Industry should take good care of the health and general welfare of those who leave school early, and it should cooperate with the government to insure that any person has the money to resume his education at any point in his life. This reform of education, says Mead, would enable people to adapt flexibly and constructively to the cultural changes that are inevitable in their lifetimes.

[5] The purpose of the general curriculum is to transmit the knowledge, skills, and values that society believes all its members should possess. The special curriculum has a number of functions, the most important of which is to educate young people for specific aspects of adult life; hence, it includes both vocational training and also preparation in such details of personal life as managing charge accounts and check books. Other functions are to prepare students for college and university entrance, to remedy backwardness in reading, writing, and arithmetic, and to develop special talents in the arts.

[6] Cf. Harold L. Hodgkinson, *Education in Social and Cultural Perspectives,* Prentice-Hall, Englewood Cliffs, New Jersey, 1962, pp. 131–137.

how to evaluate various cultural situations at the same time that he learns techniques for handling them. Under the special curriculum a future accountant might learn how to calculate the interest rate on installment-plan purchases, and under the general curriculum he might consider the ethics of installment-plan buying, together with its effects on the consumer and on the economy as a whole.[7]

The high-school curriculum, say most progressives, should pivot on the social sciences, which illuminate the contemporary world better than any other form of studies. This is especially true of courses in problems of American democracy, which deal with such contemporary matters as crime, divorce, juvenile delinquency, segregation, and so on. The social sciences also have the advantage that they are the most fluid of all areas of inquiry and so best exemplify the constantly changing nature of contemporary knowledge.

Physical science, as taught in the schools, should be in harmony with the main lines of contemporary scientific thinking. One proposal is that children should be introduced to contemporary scientific concepts and ways of thinking in the elementary rather than the high school.[8] At present, young children are inadequately prepared for the more advanced science they must tackle in the high school, since the elementary school devotes too much time to the memorization of laws and facts and too little to the methods by which they are reached. Radio and television, too, concentrate on the more spectacular offspring of technology, such as missiles and weapons, to the neglect of the scientific thinking that makes them possible.

However, if he is to acquire the world view of contemporary

---

[7] Harold L. Hodgkinson, *Education in Social and Cultural Perspectives,* Prentice-Hall, Englewood Cliffs, New Jersey, 1962, p. 137.

[8] In the words of Lawrence K. Frank, writer on anthropology with progressive sympathies:

We can, and in my judgment we should, earnestly endeavor to acquaint all students, beginning with their first year in school, with contemporary scientific ideas and assumptions, helping them to understand that to live in the contemporary world, they need this orientation because our social order, as well as our individual living, is being transformed by scientific thinking and its application in technology.

The School as Agent for Cultural Renewal, The Burton Lectures, 1958, Harvard University Press, 1959, pp. 16–18.

science, the pupil must unlearn many cherished preconceptions—about the nature of space, time, and matter, for instance—which he has absorbed during his early years, especially from his family. This unlearning should occur in the elementary school by means of what Lawrence K. Frank calls "cognitive therapy," consisting largely of group experiences that will give him the emotional support he needs if he is to abandon these assumptions and acquire a more modern scientific outlook.[9]

Finally, in the progressive view the curriculum must expand continuously. Since change multiplies the functions to be fulfilled in society and the knowledge needed to fulfill them, the school should teach new subjects as they are required.

The Conservative Solution. Conservative educators maintain that in times of rapid change education should act as a stabilizing force.[10] Although specific data and theories, in the sciences especially, may be rapidly outmoded, much knowledge retains its value and much, too, needs only to be qualified rather than abandoned. By constantly loading the curriculum with the latest and most talked-about material, we foist upon the student much that is of merely passing interest. Therefore, instead of substituting new knowledge for old we should seek as far as possible to combine the two.[11] Above all, we should never abandon proved disciplines, such as history, for the sake of newer studies, such as the social sciences, whose methods are in flux and whose data are continually disputed.

---

[9] "This can be done by group or class procedures, providing the pupil with carefully planned group experiences that will free the child from his misconceptions and help him to learn anew, finding in the group experience the reassurance and the emotional climate for giving up his previous ideas and replacing them with the new." Lawrence K. Frank, *The School as Agent for Cultural Renewal,* The Burton Lectures, 1958, Harvard University Press, 1959, p. 19.

[10] E.g., William C. Bagley, *Education and Emergent Man,* Ronald, New York, 1934, pp. 155–156.

[11] Jacques Maritain, "Thomist Views on Education," in Nelson B. Henry, ed., *Modern Philosophies and Education,* The Fifty-fourth Yearbook of the National Society for the Study of Education, University of Chicago Press, 1955, p. 70: "As concerns our changing world of knowledge . . . all new gains and discoveries should be used, not to shatter and reject what has been acquired by the past, but to augment it: a work of integration, not of destruction."

According to the conservative, the confusion of our culture does not justify confusing the child. Rather, the swifter the rate of change, the more the student requires a body of knowledge and principles that need not radically be altered, however much they may be added to or refined. What he requires above all is the habit of disciplined and systematic thought, which he can bring to any problem, no matter how novel. The liberal disciplines give him the clarity of thought, the independence of mind, and the fund of knowledge necessary for a calm and rational assessment of cultural change.[12] His intellectual development is hindered if he is required prematurely to cope with the mass of conflicting data and opinions that are pressed into service in the attempt to solve contemporary problems.[13]

Attuning the child to change by means of a focus on contempo-

---

[12] Each of these disciplines—the 3 R's, science, mathematics, history, English, and foreign languages—consists not only of a body of organized knowledge but also of the means by which such knowledge is ordered and acquired. Each represents one of the fundamental ways that the culture has developed for coming to terms with reality as the culture understands it. In Arthur Bestor's words:

They [the liberal disciplines] are the powerful tools and engines by which a man discovers and handles facts. Without the scientific and scholarly disciplines he is helpless in the presence of facts. With them he can command facts and make them serve his varied purposes. With them he can even transcend facts and deal as a rational man with the great questions of meaning and value. . . . The disciplines represent the various ways man has discovered for achieving intellectual mastery and hence practical power over the various problems that confront him.

The Restoration of Learning, Knopf, New York, 1955, pp. 34–35.

[13] *Ibid.*, pp. 134–135:

Children and young people are well aware of the violent conflicts of opinion that are abroad in the land. What they do not know, and what the school alone can show them, is that there are more orderly ways and cogent methods of gaining insight into the problems in hand than by subjecting oneself to the ceaseless battering of opposed controversialists. These methods involve the systematic accumulation of data, the mastery of techniques of analysis, the development of confidence in the handling of abstractions, and the delicate quest for objectivity and perspective. These offer no miraculous solutions, but they do offer the miracle of understanding. In a disordered world, the school can provide the student with something he can find nowhere else, a nucleus of ordered thinking about which can develop those intellectual powers that are his only enduring safeguards against frustration and hopelessness.

rary matters has other weaknesses. In the first place, it is unselective, hinging the curriculum on the state of culture rather than on principles for deciding what is worth studying in that culture. Then, too, it neglects much in the cultural heritage that is necessary for a mature insight into the present and future culture, and substitutes instead "a routine familiarity with the problems and tensions of modern living." [14] In turn, this neglect of the heritage and, hence, of cultural continuity encourages the fragmentation of knowledge. Finally, by turning itself into "a forum for the discussion of contemporary issues," the school will expose itself to the pressure of competing interest groups, each claiming a hearing in the classroom [15] for its own point of view.

The progressive emphasis on social studies has met particularly heavy criticism. David Riesman, for instance, objects that social studies divert too much time from more abstract and more intellectually rewarding subjects, and that even the content of courses in current affairs is weakened in order to meet the criticisms of local vigilantes.[16] The main conservative criticism, however, is that social studies, as the high school interprets them, fail to cultivate the power of disciplined thought, because they present facts without the theoretical principles that the pupil needs in order to comprehend them.[17]

---

[14] Thomas Molnar, *The Future of Education*, Fleet, New York, 1961, p. 72:
They [the advocates of a constantly changing curriculum] seem to take it for granted that with each invention, each gadget, each new ripple on the surface of the daily conditions of work and play, something noteworthy has come into existence, deserving not only attention but also a certain reorientation of the educational pattern. The appearance of a new technique of industrial production, new communication media, or new slogans by a social group seems to necessitate an ever–so–slight degree of curricular change so that it may not be said that education does not keep abreast of new offerings and does not encompass the whole range of modern life.

[15] Arthur Bestor, *The Restoration of Learning*, Knopf, New York, p. 71.

[16] David Riesman, *The Lonely Crowd*, Doubleday Anchor, New York, 1953, p. 99: "Thus the children are supposed to learn democracy by underplaying the skills of intellect and by overplaying the skills of gregariousness and amiability."

[17] Cf. Arthur Bestor, *The Restoration of Learning*, Knopf, New York, 1955, pp. 127–134.

Can the School Teach the Whole Culture?

The Problem. With its vast populations, its unprecedented complexity and specialization, and its growing concentration of power, modern industrial civilization has progressively reduced the scope of personal experience. As its functions call for an ever greater expertise, it increasingly restricts the range of activities in which any one man may acquire knowledge enough to participate. This fragmentation of knowledge and function threatens it with chaos. The threat is particularly acute in a democracy, where public issues are now of such a scale and complexity that a man's ordinary experiences form no criterion for appraising them. If the leaders of a democracy are chosen by an electorate with little inkling of the problems to be handled, the situation is ripe for the demagogue and the dictator. The mass media have the power to offset to a degree this shrinkage in the scope of private experience, but they have not used it sufficiently. They diffuse facts in abundance, yet these facts are relatively unassimilated, for the accepted social function of the media is not so much to educate as to entertain, to advertise, and to disseminate news and topical information. Today, it is the responsibility of education to provide the individual with an understanding of those important elements of his culture with which his experience will never directly acquaint him, and, in so doing, to give him some conception of his culture as a whole.

How is this to be done? In the modern elementary school the tendency is to synthesize knowledge. Children spend much of the time with their own teacher in their own classroom, turning to other teachers only for more specialized subjects, such as art, music, and physical education, and making use of other centers of study, such as the library, when the need arises. Instead of learning a different subject in each period, they study broad topics or problems that require them to explore and relate different areas of knowledge and experience. Through its manifold implications the problem itself diversifies the knowledge that they gather, yet at the same time it unifies this knowledge by acting as a frame of reference. In the high school the balance shifts to special subjects. With the exception of "core" programs of general education, less prominent now than a generation ago, the tendency is increasingly to study individual fields of knowledge in separate periods. Educators are far from agreed, however, that this arrangement meets the pupil's need for unified knowledge.

The Progressive Solution. The progressive proposal is to apply the approach of the elementary school more generally to the high school through the use of core curricula in general education. A core program avoids the traditional demarcations of subject matter and seeks to convey the knowledge, skills, and values necessary to the citizens of a democracy by concentrating on the main problems of the contemporary culture. Taking longer than the normal period and focusing on broad areas from which more specific problems may be selected, the core program enables students to explore many fields of knowledge and to synthesize their findings in order to solve problems that are supposed to relate directly to the conditions of their lives. The progressive educator claims that such a program enables the student to gather, organize, and unify his materials for himself and that it gives him a sense of the interrelatedness of knowledge, which is lost in the conventionally stratified curriculum.

Theodore Brameld has proposed a general curriculum unified in terms of the kinds of order in culture revealed by anthropology.[18] Brameld suggests that this curriculum should focus on human relations in three main spheres of culture: (1) family, sex, and all face-to-face relations; (2) racial, religious, class, caste, and status groups; and (3) regions, areas, nations, and systemic and whole cultures. In my view, however, it is unwise to found the order of the curriculum on a discipline so swiftly changing and so internally divided as anthropology. If such a program is to be more integrated than the traditional academic curriculum, it must unify its different elements in terms of broad configurations of culture, on which, as Brameld admits, anthropologists themselves are not in agreement. Brameld also suggests ordering this curriculum about those cross-cultural regularities already discovered by anthropologists. As we have seen, however (pp. 30–31), these regularities, even insofar as they meet with general agreement, are still too vague to provide a framework for the curriculum.

---

[18] Theodore Brameld, *Cultural Foundations of Education*, Harper, New York, 1957, pp. 74–76.

The Conservative Solution. Contrary to the progressive view, conservative educators maintain that contemporary culture is too vast and too complex to be understood through an investigation of its various problems. Before he can tackle such problems, the student must first grasp the general principles of the different fields of knowledge into which the phenomena of nature and culture have been divided for purposes of investigation—the principles, that is, of the major intellectual disciplines.[19] These principles together form a consistent world view for ordering the events and processes of culture both now and in the immediate future.

Conservatives agree with progressives on the need for a unified curriculum to counteract the current fragmentation of knowledge and culture, but they criticize core curricula and other allegedly integrated courses of study as makeshift attempts to put together the cultural whole that educators already have shattered if they permit the child to learn in accordance with his own interests. Mistakenly, the progressives have attempted "to produce a synthesis of knowledge before there is any analyzed and ordered knowledge to integrate."[20] To integrate knowledge, one must bring to a problem both organized information and disciplined powers of mind. Yet, nearly all integrated courses in high school and many in college present the problems but not the organized information or the mental discipline. The student is expected to synthesize cultural materials without ever having learned to analyze them. "They [integrated courses] confront a student with the same unanalyzed problems that life confronts him with and they ask him to seek a solution by using his own undeveloped mental abilities. . . . They propose—contrary to all reason and experience—to train men to perform the culminating acts of thought while skipping all the antecedent stages." The school's real function, writes Arthur Bestor,

---

[19] E.g., John Wild, "Education and Human Society: A Realist View," in Nelson B. Henry, ed., *Modern Philosophies and Education*, The Fifty-fourth Yearbook of the National Society for the Study of Education, Chicago, University of Chicago Press, 1955, p. 27: "Genuine, stable integration of the whole culture can be attained only by universal principles grounded on observation."

[20] Arthur Bestor, *The Restoration of Knowledge*, Knopf, New York, 1959, p. 59.

. . . is to aid the young man to stand temporarily aloof from a complex problem while he analyzes it and works out the strategy of dealing with its various elements. In this process of analysis the separate disciplines play an indispensable role. They break down the involved situations of life into separate problems susceptible of handling by powerful specialized methods. They provide the techniques that can be employed in a rational, coordinated attack upon the original question.[21]

Conservatives believe that education should proceed in distinct stages. In the elementary school the child's experience is largely undifferentiated, but the teacher should gradually lead him to analyze this experience into manageable elements. The secondary school explores these elements systematically through the different disciplines. No integrated course should come before the senior year of high school—or, for those who go there, before college. An integrated course is actually very difficult, since it requires the student to comprehend essential differences between disciplines, to see how each discipline is appropriate to the particular fields of experience that it investigates, and to transfer concepts from one discipline to another. This, in turn, requires a firm grasp of some of the ways of thinking involved, considerable insight, and a developed capacity to generalize—in short, intellectual maturity. Since they begin when the pupil is intellectually too immature, integrated courses in the high school today generally tend to survey facts rather than to investigate the means by which facts are discovered and organized. They fail conspicuously to train disciplined thinking.

Educating the Culturally Disadvantaged

The Problem. Educating the culturally disadvantaged has long been a problem in this country, but two factors in particular have given it special importance in recent years. One is the continuing trend to urbanization; the other is the decay of city centers, which has been caused by an exodus of the white middle class to the suburbs and an influx of rural poor, many of them Negro and Spanish-speaking.[22] Every year 50,000 whites leave New York;

---

21 *Ibid.*, pp. 60–61.
22 Clemmont E. Vontress, "Our Demoralizing Slum Schools," *Phi Delta Kappan*, XLV, No. 2 (November 1963), 77.

15,000, Chicago; and 3,000, Cleveland. Meantime, Negroes and Puerto Ricans pour into New York, Mexicans into Los Angeles, and Negroes and Appalachian whites into the big cities of the North and Middle West. In the hearts of these cities housing is generally bad, population density high, and privacy minimal.[23] Many of the inhabitants are on public relief. Most have scanty education and little vocational competence. Families are disorganized and crime flourishes, especially among the young.

Who are the culturally disadavantaged pupils? They are generally from the lower classes and are academically backward, the second characteristic being generally, though not always, a consequence of the first. Their parents have been unable to give them the background and preparation necessary for formal learning, which the middle-class parent imparts to his children as a matter of course. Since their parents often do work that requires little education, the children frequently underestimate the school's capacity to prepare them for life. Coming, as they do, from depressed areas and often from broken homes, they have little feeling that society as a whole cares for them. Consequently, they often experience great difficulty in adapting to the outside world as well as to schools permeated by middle-class values. They tend to be more aggressive and insecure than other children; they are more prone to neuroses and sometimes to complete breakdowns; and they turn more readily to delinquency. Many of them fail to master the normal academic curriculum (another blow to their already faltering self-esteem), many drop out of school, and few find their way to college. They are further set back by their tendency to move from one neighborhood and school to another, disturbing their own education as well as that of their less mobile fellows.[24]

In 1950, in the public schools of the nation's fourteen largest

---

23 Negro population density in the big cities of the North and Middle West is now four times that of whites. Detroit is 28.9 per cent Negro, Chicago 22.9 per cent, and Washington, D.C., 53.9 per cent. *Ibid.*

24 In Manhattan, where the elementary schools are more than 76 per cent Negro and Puerto Rican, the turnover in a recent year was 51 per cent, and in three almost wholly Negro schools it reached 100 per cent. Frederick Shaw, "Educating Culturally Deprived Youth in Urban Centers," *Phi Delta Kappan*, XLV, No. 2 (November 1963), p. 93.

cities about one child in ten was culturally disadvantaged; in 1960 one in three; and in 1970 it may be one in two. The proportion varies from one school to another.[25] Where the culturally disadvantaged constitute 90 per cent or more of the enrollment, the whole school may need a special program of studies. In most schools, however, where the ratio may be from one in three to one in ten, teachers face the threefold problem of arranging a program for only part of the student body (generally distributed through all grades), deciding which particular students should qualify for this program, and finding a title for the program that will indicate its purpose without in any way denigrating it.[26]

Programs for the Culturally Disadvantaged. How are we to raise the culturally disadvantaged child to middle-class standards of educational achievement? The first program to deal specifically with this problem was the Guidance Demonstration Project in New York City in 1956, later expanded and renamed Higher Horizons. The latter, in turn, inspired a host of other programs, including the Ford Foundation's Great Cities Grey Areas programs and the first statewide program, Project ABLE, begun by New York State in 1961.[27] Although it has been argued that these programs could concentrate more effectively on the elementary grades, they are, in fact, operating successfully at all levels.[28] Thus, before a school introduces one of these programs, the main question it must decide is not the grade level on which to focus but rather the grade level at which to begin, which will depend, in turn, on the school's facilities, the preparedness of its staff, the

[25] Indeed, the last ratio already has been reached in Washington, D.C., Baltimore, Wilmington, and Philadelphia. Bernard A. Kaplan, "Issues in Educating the Culturally Disadvantaged," *ibid.*, p. 71.
[26] Such titles include Higher Horizons, Project ABLE, Operation Bootstrap, Springboard, New Frontiers, Wings, Project Mercury, Project HELP, Talent Demonstration. Bernard A. Kaplan, "Issues in Educating the Culturally Disadvantaged," *Phi Delta Kappan*, XLV, No. 2 (November 1963), p. 71.
[27] Similar programs are now being planned or considered by four other states: Maine, Rhode Island, Pennsylvania, and California.
[28] In New York State there are Project ABLE programs at all levels, although most of them focus on grades four through eight, and the Higher Horizons program now covers all grades from three to ten. A few colleges, such as Brown Community College in New York City, are experimenting with special preadmission programs for culturally disadvantaged students.

resources of the community, and the support of parents. Nor is there a standard program suitable for every community. Each school must design its own program in accordance with local needs and local leadership, although most programs will share certain basic likenesses. Nevertheless, each community can exchange visits and information with other communities running similar programs, and all can learn from the research and program reports that are steadily mounting up.[29]

Basically, these programs succeed to the extent that they persuade the culturally disadvantaged pupil that the school is taking an interest in him personally and so stimulate him to cooperate with his teachers and to aim at a higher level of achievement. Indeed, many agencies report that academic progress has been preceded by positive changes in the student's behavior, such as better speech and dress, regular attendance, and greater interest in his studies.

These programs concentrate on teaching the culturally disadvantaged child the basic intellectual skills—reading, writing, and simple arithmetic—before turning to more advanced subjects like algebra, geometry, literature, and foreign languages.[30] Reading, in particular, receives special attention. In New York's Demonstration Guidance project, for example, all teachers, whatever their subjects, devote the first ten minutes of each period to reading.[31] Advocates urge that each classroom should have its own library on open shelves and that books should be readily available throughout the school.[32]

Generally, it is assumed that these children cannot concentrate on abstract academic topics, such as multiplication tables or English grammar, unless these topics are made relevant to their daily lives. Classes, then, tend to take as their point of departure

---

29 For example, no two programs in Project ABLE are exactly alike, although all were planned and inaugurated during 1961 under the auspices of the State Education Department. Bernard A. Kaplan, *op. cit.*, p. 74.

30 David P. Ausubel, "A Teaching Strategy for Culturally Deprived Pupils: Cognitive and Motivational Considerations," *The School Review*, Winter, 1963, pp. 460–461.

31 Frederick Shaw, "Educating Culturally Deprived Youth in Urban Centers," *Phi Delta Kappan*, XLV, No. 2 (November 1963), p. 94.

32 Clemmont E. Vontress, "Our Demoralizing Slum Schools," *ibid.*, p. 81.

the circumstances under which these children live and the problems that they encounter. Textbooks and other teaching materials also are adapted to these conditions. The culturally deprived child usually sees his parents in work clothes, tired from the day and often irritable. His mother, if not herself a wage earner, generally is burdened with the chores of the house and with the care of a large, unruly family. Yet, in the past, most textbooks have portrayed immaculate Anglo American parents taking their ease with happy, well-behaved children on the barbered lawns of middle class homes. Therefore, textbooks and readers are being developed whose motifs are slums, not suburbs, and whose characters come from a range of ethnic backgrounds.

Schools also seek to enlist the support of the parents. Recent immigrants from the rural South or Puerto Rico know little of urban living and the demands that it makes on their children. Many lack either knowledge or awareness of the educational and cultural opportunities available Counselors seek to persuade such parents to encourage their children to study, and to allow them time and privacy to do so. Schools spend much time setting up workshops, meeting and interviewing parents, and even arranging trips for them.[33]

They also try to integrate the child into his immediate community, helping him to plan his career and to find a job. They arrange trips to factories, libraries, museums, theaters, concerts, the ballet, and colleges. As a result, students become interested in the arts and are no longer abashed at listening to classical music or reading quality paperbacks.[34]

An Appraisal of These Programs. Programs for the culturally disadvantaged raise a number of theoretical issues. First, how far should the curriculum correspond to the pupils' current concerns and problems in life adjustment? Undoubtedly one of the main purposes of these programs is to stimulate the pupil's desire to learn by providing a curriculum clearly related to the conditions in which he lives. On the other hand, it is also possible to underestimate his capacity for an interest in learning as such. Despite

---

[33] Cf. Ruth Landes, *Culture in American Education,* chapter on counseling, Wiley, New York, in press.
[34] Frederick Shaw, *op. cit.,* p. 95.

an unpropitious home background, if he is enthusiastically taught, successful learning may of itself generate the motive for further learning.[35] In the conservative view, then, which in this case is not limited to conservative educators alone, these programs could be intellectually more ambitious and concentrate more heavily on the acquisition of academic subject matter.

Second, by beginning at a lower than average intellectual level, do these programs reinforce the disparity between the standards of lower- and middle-class education? Not in the long run, for their intention is to ground the pupil thoroughly in the fundamentals in order to prepare him for the study of more sophisticated subjects. Unless the culturally disadvantaged pupil receives extra attention at the very outset of his educational career, the deficiencies in his environment, which have slowed his intellectual development, cause him to experience progressively greater difficulty with a curriculum designed for middle-class children.[36]

Next, are these programs fair to other children? [37] It is argued that all the attractions of the special programs—the extra teachers and counselors, the special services and supplies, the many trips— arouse the envy of students, teachers, administrators, and parents at schools that lack these projects, and especially at schools where the program serves only part of the student body. It is also objected that these programs are unfair to other children because they cost more per pupil.

These objections may be countered with a number of arguments. To begin, the principle that special educational problems merit

---

[35] Cf. David P. Ausubel, "A Teaching Strategy for Culturally Deprived Pupils: Cognitive and Motivational Considerations," *The School Review,* Winter, 1963, pp. 460–461.

[36] David P. Ausubel, *ibid.,* p. 465:

It [beginning at the pupil's actual state of readiness] is merely a necessary first step in preparing him to cope with more advanced subject matter, and hence in eventually reducing existing social class differentials in academic achievement. To set the same initial standards and expectations for the academically retarded culturally deprived child as for the non-retarded middle-or-lower class child is automatically to insure the former's failure and to widen prevailing discrepancies between social class groups.

[37] Cf. Bernard A. Kaplan "Issues in Educating the Culturally Disadvantaged," *Phi Delta Kappan,* XLV, No. 2 (November 1963), pp. 71–74.

special programs at extra cost has already been accepted in the case of physically handicapped, mentally retarded, academically gifted, and emotionally disturbed children. Secondly, if culturally deprived children are to have the same educational opportunity as other children, the only way to compensate for the deficiencies in their upbringing and surroundings is to give them more attention in the school. Furthermore, whatever their extra cost, these programs save the community money in the long run, because, by reducing dropouts especially, they produce more competent and productive citizens and help to lower expenditures on welfare, unemployment benefits, and rehabilitation.

Fourth, do such programs help to perpetuate segregation in fact, if not in name? Most of them serve children who come almost entirely from minority groups and who attend schools that, on account of housing patterns, cater to what are *de facto* segregated neighborhoods.[38] It is felt by some, then, that the more such programs succeed, the more likely people are to accept the existence of segregated schools serving segregated neighborhoods. One may reply, however, that these programs actually mitigate segregation, since they enable students to take part in activities with

---

[38] Although in the North no child is refused admission to a school on grounds of race or color, nonwhite children frequently attend wholly or predominantly nonwhite schools because it is virtually impossible for their parents to obtain accommodation in white neighborhoods. *De facto* segregation is most widespread in neighborhood elementary schools but much less so in high schools, which are often large enough to cut across housing patterns. In 1960, New York City began a policy of "open enrollment," permitting nonwhite children to apply for transfer to selected mainly white schools, with the result that nearly 15,000 children are now attending open enrollment schools out of their neighborhoods. However, although this policy integrates the transferred children, it does not desegregate any further the schools from which they come. See Fred M. Hechinger, "Integration Problems in the North," *New York Times*, Western Edition, January 15, 1964, p. 8. According to Mayer and Holt, sociologists at Wayne State University, racial segregation in housing is actually increasing in most Northern industrial cities. They claim for instance, that in 1960 23 per cent of the Negro population in Detroit lived in Negro ghettos, 7.2 per cent more than in 1930. Albert J. Mayer and Thomas F. Holt, *Time*, November 9, 1962, p. 62. Cited by Virgil A. Clift, "Factors Relating to the Education of Culturally Deprived Negro Youth," *Educational Theory*, XIV, No. 2 (April 1964), pp. 77–78.

children from the entire school district and, indeed, qualify some for academic and honors courses in the high school, where they can mix more intimately with white middle-class children. Moreover, such programs may eventually serve as magnets attracting white middle-class pupils and thus contributing to desegregation.

Finally, are these programs effective because of their specific content, or because they make their students feel that they are receiving special attention? If the students work better because they have been motivated to do so, are there other more effective or less costly methods of achieving the same result? It is suggested that these programs could be cut down to one or two features and still achieve the same objectives. On the other hand, since motivation and underachievement are highly complex phenomena, simplified programs are, in fact, likely to motivate fewer students. Indeed, even the full Higher Horizons programs, with their wide range of activities, have failed to improve the performance of some students.[39]

THE TEACHER IN THE CONTEMPORARY CULTURE

It is now time to consider two aspects of the relation of the teacher to American culture and American education. First, what is his standing in this culture? Second, what authority does this culture allow him to exercise over his pupils?

The Status of the Teacher

As modern industrial society becomes more specialized, it must continually improve the education of the majority of its members in order to insure that they can perform the roles it expects of them. A better educated populace requires more highly trained, and hence more specialized, teachers. As teaching grows in specialization and importance to society, it becomes in a sense more professionalized, since teachers must now be both more knowledgeable and more conscious of their responsibility to the community. Yet, there is general agreement that the American teacher

---

[39] Cf. Bernard A. Kaplan "Issues in Educating the Culturally Disadvantaged," *Phi Delta Kappan*, XLV, No. 2 (November 1963), p. 74.

in the twentieth century is not technically a professional at all.[40] Why is this so?

In the first place, a profession should control not only the training but also the conduct of its members. Yet, American teachers are neither certified nor, in the broadest sense, supervised by master teachers. Public departments or boards of education prescribe the courses that an intending teacher must take; they also issue his certificate, pay him, and grant him his tenure. Matters of conduct are settled by state and local boards of education composed mainly of laymen.

A professional person should also be able to make important decisions. The teacher, however, is little more than a cog in the wheel of mass education. Unlike big business, which requires its executives to exercise initiative, mass education allows the teacher little scope of his own. As one commentator has said:

He [the teacher] was demoted to an employee on the bottom link of a long chain of command which winds its way from the state governor's office and the chambers of the state legislature to state boards and state education departments, further down to local school boards and offices of superintendents, and from them to the principals of individual schools.[41]

The board of education, for instance, usually decides what subjects shall be taught and with what textbooks, and very often the principal promotes pupils and assigns them to their classes.

The teacher's independence is also restricted by the growing multitude of educational specialists, such as counselors, super-

---

[40] Bernard Barker "Some Problems in the Sociology of the Professions," *Daedalus*, The Professions, XCII, No. 4 (Fall 1963), p. 672:

Professional behavior may be defined in terms of four essential attributes; a high degree of generalized and systematic knowledge; primary orientation to the community interest rather than to individual self-interest; a high degree of self-control of behavior through codes of ethics internalized in the process of work socialization and through voluntary associations organized and operated by the work specialists themselves; and a system of rewards (monetary and honorary) that is primarily a set of symbols of work achievement and thus ends in themselves, not means to some end of individual self-interest.

[41] Alma S. Wittlin, "The Teacher," *Daedalus*, The Professions, XCII, No. 4 (Fall 1963), p. 752.

visors, and statisticians. These specialists are necessary, yet they narrow the number of things that a teacher can decide. On the other hand, there is little doubt that if teachers and specialists were to work more as a team, they could pursue their respective tasks without infringing on, and hence impoverishing, the labors of each, as is too often the case at present.[42]

Finally, whereas the professional man enjoys high social esteem, the teacher, with the exception of the university professor, is little regarded. The man in the street, who would not dream of arguing with his doctor or lawyer in matters of professional knowledge and competence, feels quite free to criticize the decisions of teachers.

Naturally, educators would like to raise their professional standing.[43] One way is for teachers to have a greater voice in the selection of their colleagues. Another is to improve the quality of teachers, although this proposal encounters the objection that it would reduce the number of teachers to be certified at a time when the number of pupils and the length of their education are both increasing. Yet, even these practical steps seem hardly likely to attain the end that their protagonists set them. Surely education will not become a profession, in the sense that law and medicine are professions, until the public learn to respect knowledge *as such*. For is this not the teacher's chief stock in trade?

The Authority of the Teacher

At the turn of the century the roles of parent and teacher were sharply divided. The teacher was expected to train the intellect and teach decorum. It was his privilege to develop a personal interest in his pupils, but only informally. Gradually the teacher's function has expanded, until today he attends almost as much to his pupils' emotional experiences as to their intellectual ones. He takes an interest, for example, in their choice of friends, their out-of-school pursuits, and their social and psychological adjustment. At the same time, the social distance between teacher and

---

[42] Cf. *ibid.*
[43] Cf. George Z. F. Bereday and Joseph A. Lauwerys ed., "The Education and Training of Teachers," *The Year Book of Education*, 1963, Harcourt, Brace and World, New York, 1963.

pupil has narrowed. If the modern teacher has ceased to inspire the awe or veneration of his predecessor, he has nevertheless become more flexible, more understanding, and more formally attentive to his students, who, in turn, enjoy more freedom of speech and exercise greater initiative. On the other hand, he has surrendered much of his influence to the peer group and many of his responsibilities to various educational specialists. The errors to which he is prone are no longer remoteness from his pupils and lack of sympathy but rather the tendency to value comradeship and affection at the expense of learning and to equate chaos and disorder with democracy in the classroom.

Traditionally, the teacher has been regarded as the conserver of cultural tradition. His duty has been to pass on whatever elements of the culture's experience seemed important enough to be preserved. Progressive education, however, challenges this view. For progressivism the teacher's task is partly to preserve, but partly also to disturb, the traditions of culture by assisting the young to think critically for themselves about the problems of the contemporary world.

The progressive teacher believes that if the pupil has a problem to solve which genuinely interests him, he tends to cooperate more with his teacher and classmates. The teacher, then, should be a guide who helps the exploring student solve the problems that he encounters by advising him how to acquire the knowledge and skills to do so. Ideally, he places his greater knowledge and experience at the pupil's disposal, so that the latter has available those elements of culture that he needs in order to solve his problems—elements that, unassisted, he would either not have found or would have acquired only with much unprofitable labor and loss of time. Instead of telling his pupils what to study, the teacher plans their courses of study with them. To do so, he creates an informal classroom in which pupils express themselves freely and, on appropriate occasions, actually criticize him. In the progressive view, this kind of teaching is both more demanding and more fruitful than the type of teaching that prearranges the pupil's studies without consulting him.

Critics of progressivism deplore this expansion of the teacher's interests on the grounds that it encourages pupils to be anti-intellectual and conformist. Instead of acquiring mental discipline, pupils learn how to "get on" with one another, a process that generally entails adjustment of the pupil to the group rather than a cooperation of equal individuals. In David Riesman's words, the teacher increasingly is trained to be "more concerned with the child's social and psychological adjustment than with his academic progress—indeed, to scan the intellectual performance for signs of maladjustment." Consequently, he conveys to the children that "what matters is not their industry or learning as such but their adjustment in the group, their cooperation, their (carefully stylized and limited) initiative and leadership." [44]

According to most critics of progressivism, the teacher should not be a guide on whom the student calls but rather an instructor to whom he listens. It is the teacher who should decide what and how much the student shall learn. But this by no means absolves him of all responsibility to consult the student's interests. Unlike the progressive, however, for whom such interests form the main criterion of what the child should learn, the conservative educator believes that the matter to be learned should be the criterion of what interests to arouse in the child.

Discipline. Turning to the question of discipline, we find that the first child-centered schools of the progressive movement encouraged the pupil to discipline himself by the simple expedient of letting him study whatever aroused his interests. This approach to discipline, however, soon gave way to the view that the class or the learning group should choose and maintain its own standards of behavior. In the progressive school, the students, in consultation with their teacher, discuss and then vote on certain rules of procedure for attaining the goals that have brought them together. Such discipline is said to be democratic, because the students have chosen it themselves and may modify it at any time—under appropriate guidance.

Jules Henry commends progressivism for advocating a relatively permissive and informal atmosphere.[45] Children, he says, are at ease with their teacher when they can make suggestions to him

44 David Riesman, *The Lonely Crowd*, Doubleday Anchor, New York, 1953, pp. 60, 62.
45 Jules Henry, "A Cross-Cultural Survey of Education," *Current Anthropology*, I, No. 4 (July 1960), pp. 285–286.

about the conduct of the lesson, move about the class and approach him physically, and on occasions even call him by his first name. The teacher relaxes them by moving about the room himself, letting them approach him, and often addressing them by their nicknames; also by being sensitive to their feelings, accepting their outbursts of emotion, and responding to cues, such as frowns or smiles, without waiting for questions or raised hands.

Critics of progressivism are disturbed by what they consider a drastic decline in the institutional authority of the teacher—that is, the authority he derives from his professional role rather than from his personal qualities. This decline is partly the result of the increasing rate of cultural change, which, in the child's eyes, calls into question the superior knowledge and experience on which this authority used to be based. But, say the critics, it is also a decline that has been aided and abetted by the progressive-inspired transfer of the responsibility for discipline from the teacher to the pupils themselves.

Admittedly, the teacher has, in a sense, acquired more power over his pupils, since education increasingly is becoming the key to good jobs and social prestige. Yet, this power is no substitute for the authority that he has lost. Those who defer to him do so mostly because they see in him a source of knowledge and skills, which they wish to acquire. Those who do not, become apathetic to learning or retire into the anti-intellectual subculture of adolescent. Thus, to maintain order the teacher is forced to manipulate his pupils as far as he can from the insecure position of an "opinion leader" or "resource person." [46]

Critics reject the progressive principle that the learning group should discipline itself. Although he is sympathetic to progressive education, Jules Henry disagrees with Melford Spiro that the informality of the high schools in the Israeli *kibbutzim* reflects the lack of social distance between teacher and pupil. [47] (In these schools children leave the room at will, address the teacher by

---

[46] This criticism has been expressed by, for example, Jean Floud, "Teaching in the Affluent Society," in George Z. F. Bereday and Joseph A. Lauwerys, eds., "The Education and Training of Teachers," *The Year Book of Education,* 1963, Harcourt, Brace and World, New York, 1963, pp. 382–389.

[47] See Melford E. Spiro, *Children of the Kibbutz,* Harvard University Press, 1958, pp. 363–364.

his first name, and criticize him when they feel he is wrong.) Henry points out that in primitive societies, where teacher and pupil are generally very close indeed, there is no such informality when children are being instructed in the heritage of the culture.[48] He suggests that, in fact, the excessive informality of many Israeli and American schools stems from the teacher's deliberate refusal to establish a clear source of authority in the classroom, so that the children are often unsure where to draw the line in their behavior and whom precisely to heed, whether the teacher or one of their own number.

For the first time in the history of our culture teachers are encouraging children to release their impulses rather than to control them. "Spontaneity," "freedom," and "permissiveness" are all names given to this process.[49] Yet, this approach puts the teacher in a dilemma. How can he help the child release his impulses and yet inculcate subject matter? How can he transmit the heritage unless his pupils are attentive enough to receive it?

Teachers come to terms in different ways with the diminution in their authority. Jules Henry vividly depicts two methods adopted, though not in conscious response to this phenomenon, in the primary schools of middle-class suburbs.[50] One, used by women, is to enfold the class in affection and then play on the children's fear of losing this affection in order to hold their attention; the other, used by one male teacher whom Henry investigated, is to become a "buddy daddy" to the children—a jocular, enthusiastic combination of daddy and big brother, who seeks to keep control through a refusal to rouse the "anti" feelings sometimes stimulated by an authoritarian personality.

Granted that these methods have been examined only in middle-

[48] Jules Henry, "A Cross-Cultural Survey of Education," *Current Anthropology*, I, No. 4 (July 1960), pp. 285–286 (italics in original): "Though in primitive cultures the social distance between teacher and pupil is, with certain exceptions . . . very small, I have not found in primitive culture such generalized random behavior *when the children are receiving systematic instruction in cultural skills.*"

[49] Cf. Jules Henry, *Culture Against Man*, Random House, New York, 1963, p. 305.

[50] Jules Henry, "Spontaneity, Initiative, and Creativity in Suburban Classrooms," in George D. Spindler, ed., *Education and Culture: Anthropological Approaches*, Holt, Rinehart and Winston, New York, 1963, pp. 215–233.

class schools, yet in an increasingly affluent society the norms of the middle class seem likely to spread progressively through the population. But, adopted *ad hoc* and unguided by any theory about what education should achieve, such methods may do much harm. The teacher trades his authority for popularity and gets, in return, mostly peace of mind (and not always that). However this exchange may benefit the teacher psychologically, it can be justified educationally only if it leads to the attainment of certain ends prescribed by theory as related to observed practice.

In the conservative view, children will allow themselves to be controlled by teachers whom they respect. If any teacher ceases to lead, the class becomes confused and order breaks down. If, on the other hand, he becomes merely autocratic, they resent and frustrate him. The teacher must see that the controls placed on his pupils are fair, or they will not be internalized and self-discipline will not be attained. In short, if children are to learn how to control themselves, they need limits that they can respect and teachers with whom they can identify.

One way to enhance the prestige and authority of the teacher is to attract more men into the profession, especially at the elementary-school level. Another way is to shorten hours of work, so that men may spend more time at home. Both should lead to a resurgence in masculine authority, not only in the school but also in the family. The youth of America cannot but benefit, for not only do men by and large treat children less sentimentally than women, but boys need men to imitate and girls need the mature guidance and counsel that older men can offer.

In this chapter I have considered two very broad topics: (1) the interaction of contemporary American culture with the public-school curriculum, and (2) the influence of this culture on the teacher's standing in the community and on his authority in the classroom. Under (1) I discussed three problems: What curriculum best suits the highly dynamic character of American culture? Can the school teach the whole of this culture? How should we educate the culturally disadvantaged?

The essence of the first problem is that in a swiftly changing culture it is difficult to know what knowledge and skills to teach, since at least some of what is imparted to a given generation of students may no longer be important to the culture a decade hence.

Progressive educators argue that the best way to solve this problem is to keep the curriculum as up to date as possible by focusing on the main concerns of the contemporary culture. Conservative educators, on the other hand, maintain that the very confusion of contemporary culture makes it the more important to find and to teach those items of knowledge and those skills that are not likely to lose their importance with cultural change.

The heart of the second problem is that the growing complexity of today's culture is rapidly transforming us all into specialists with little knowledge of areas of culture outside our own. How is the school to counter this fragmentation of knowledge and function? Progressive educators advocate the study of "core" problems relating to broad sectors of the culture and requiring the student to select knowledge from a range of subject matter. Conservative educators reply that the student must first master the major intellectual disciplines if he is to make any sense of the complexity of cultural materials.

The third problem is the need to raise the cultural level of children from poor families—many of them Negro or Spanish-speaking—to the national average. Most educators solve this problem by constructing curricula geared to the students' cultural background, with special emphasis on such basic skills as reading.

The development of our culture also involves the authority and standing of teachers. Whether or not one believes that the authority of the teacher has declined will depend on one's view of the kind of authority that the teacher should have. His present precarious condition is, in large measure, the result of the more permissive upbringing now preferred by parents, affected as they are by an increasingly affluent society. (A richer, more hedonistic generation indulges its children more than it was indulged itself.) It is also partly the result of the persistent campaign of progressive education for more flexible methods of classroom control, although, as one astute critic has remarked, such permissiveness and flexibility can become just as much a form of controlled behavior as authoritarianism itself.[51]

---

[51] Fred Kerlinger, "The Implication of the Permissiveness Doctrine in American Education," in Hobert W. Burns and Charles J. Brauner, *Philosophy of Education*, Ronald, New York, 1962, pp. 381–396.

The fundamental reason why the teacher's standing is low relative to the social importance of his occupation is that, on the whole, our culture, while respecting knowledge, does not properly recognize the teacher as one of its major agents. Seldom rewarded for his excellence to the extent of persons in comparable occupations, and therefore lacking their tangible manifestations of success, the teacher mistakenly is thought to lack their merit. Ironically the best way to cope with the difficulty is, through education itself, to demonstrate the crucial importance of the cultural role of our educational system and to provide greater rewards for those who are concerned with it. For the life of a culture can be no healthier than the education that sustains it.

References

Benedict, Ruth, *Patterns of Culture*, Houghton Mifflin, Boston, 1934.
Benedict, Ruth, "Continuities and Discontinuities in Cultural Conditioning," in W. Martin and C. Stendler, eds., *Readings in Child Development*, Harcourt, Brace, New York, 1954, pp. 142–148.
Bidney, David, *Theoretical Anthropology*, Columbia University Press, New York, 1953.
Brameld, Theodore, *Cultural Foundations of Education*, Harper, New York, 1957.
Coleman, James S., *The Adolescent Society*, Free Press of Glencoe, New York, 1961.
Durkheim, Emile, *Education and Society*, Sherwood D. Fox, trans., Free Press of Glencoe, New York, 1956.
Durkheim, Emile, *Moral Education: A Study in the Theory and Application of the Study of Education*, Everett K. Wilson and Herman Schnurer, trans., Free Press of Glencoe, New York, 1961.
Frank, Lawrence K., *The School as Agent for Cultural Renewal*, The Burton Lectures, 1958, Harvard University Press, 1959.
Gruber, Frederick C., ed., *Anthropology and Education*, University of Pennsylvania Press, 1961.
Henry, Jules, "A Cross-Cultural Outline of Education," *Current Anthropology*, I, No. 4 (July 1960), 267–305.
Henry, Jules, *Culture Against Man*, Random House, New York, 1963.
Herskovits, Melville J., *Cultural Anthropology*, Knopf, New York, 1955.
Hodgkinson, Harold L., *Education in Social and Cultural Perspectives*, Prentice-Hall, Englewood Cliffs, New Jersey, 1962.
Kaplan, Bert, ed., *Studying Personality Cross-Culturally*, Row, Peterson, Evanston, Illinois, 1961.

Kluckhohn, Clyde, *Mirror for Man: The Relation of Anthropology to Modern Life,* Whittlesey House, New York, 1949.
Kluckhohn, Clyde, Henry A. Murray, David M. Schneider, eds., *Personality in Nature, Society, and Culture,* Knopf, New York, 1959.
Kroeber, A. L., *The Nature of Culture,* University of Chicago Press, 1952.
Landes, Ruth, *Culture in American Education,* Wiley, New York, in press.
Lee, Dorothy, *Freedom and Culture,* Prentice-Hall, Englewood Cliffs, New Jersey, 1959.
Mead, Margaret, *Male and Female,* Morrow, New York, 1949.
Mead, Margaret, *Coming of Age in Samoa,* American Library, New York, 1950.
Spindler, George D., ed., *The Transmission of American Culture,* The Burton Lectures, 1957, Harvard University Press, 1959.
Spindler, George D., ed., *Education and Culture: Anthropological Approaches,* Holt, Rinehart and Winston, New York, 1963.
Wallace, Anthony F. C., *Culture and Personality,* Random House, New York, 1961.
White, Leslie A., *The Science of Culture,* Farrar, Straus, New York, 1949.
Whiting, Beatrice B., ed., *Six Cultures: Studies of Child Rearing,* Wiley, New York, 1963.

Index

Adler, Mortimer J., 40n
Adolescent, the modern, 101–103;
 see also Children
Adults, in American culture, 97–102
 in primitive societies, 97–101
Adventists, Seventh-Day, 71
Africa, 45
 South, 92
Allport, Gordon, 50, 59n, 60n, 61
 approach to personality and cul-
 ture, 63
America, 1, 45; see also United States
American culture, 8; see also Culture
American Indian, 53, 71; see also
 Indians
Animal rationale, 47
Animal symbolicum, 47
Anomie, 117
Anthropologists, education and, 90–
 94
Anthropology, education and, 11–16
 the meaning of, 1–3
Apollonian ethos, 6, 55
Arabs, 9
Arapesh society, 95
Aristotelian logic, 48
Arizona, 53
Ascham, Roger, 69
Ausubel, David P., 130n, 149n, 151n
Authority, the teacher and, 155–162;
 see also Teacher
Aztec, 67n; see also Indians

Bagby, Philip H. 23n, 27
Bagley, William C., 65n, 140n
Barker, Bernard, 154n
Barnett, H. G., 8n
Beaglehole, Ernest, 85n
Benedict, Ruth, 2, 5–6, 31, 34n, 55,
 91, 98n, 99n, 104, 105, 109,
 163
 and *ethos*, 5–6
 on discontinuity, 104
 on education, 91
Bereday, George Z. F., 107n, 119n,
 137n, 155n
Berkson, I. B., 133
Bestor, Arthur, 141n, 142n, 145
Bidney, David, 22, 27, 33, 34n, 39,
 40n, 163
Boas, Franz, 2, 22, 31, 44n, 104n
Bourgeois, 57
Brameld, Theodore, 15, 36, 87, 88,
 163
 on the school curriculum, 144
 reconstructionism and cultural
 change, 87–90
Brauner, Charles J., 161n
Breed, Frederick, 65n
Brickman, William W., 65n
British anthropology, 2
Broudy, Harry S., 133
Brown, Ina Corrine, 44n, 96n
Bruner, Jerome S., 113
Burns, Hobert W., 161n